MOTHER OF WRITING

Ancient Hymns for Seshat

BY CHELSEA LUELLON BOLTON

Dedication

To Seshat in all Her names, forms, and aspects.

Figure 1: The Goddess Seshat.

Contents

Hymns to Seshat
In Her Name of Sefkhet Abwy

Hymns of Seshat Syncretisms

Appendixes

Acknowledgements

Thank you to Rev. Dr. Tamara L. Siuda for giving me permission to include her material from the *Ancient Egyptian Prayerbook, The Ancient Egyptian Daybook* and *Nebt-Het: Lady of the House.*

Thank you to Dr. Dagmar Budde for granting permission to include my translations from his work, <u>Die Göttin Seschat</u>.

Thank you to IFAO for granting permission to include material from *Les Inscriptions du Temple d'Opet a Karnak III: Traduction integrale des textes rituels-Essai d'interpretation* and *Komir. I. - The Discovery of Komir Temple. Preliminary Report. II. - Deux hymnes aux divinites de Komir : Anoukis et Nephthys.*

Thank you to Verlag der Österreichischen Akademie der Wissenschaften | Austrian Academy of Sciences Press for granting permission to include material from *Philae III: Die Zweite Ostkolonnade des Tempels der Isis in Philae. (CO II und CO II K).*

Thank you to Dr. Barbara A. Richter for granting permission to include her work from <u>The Theology of Hathor of Dendera: Aural and Visual Scribal Techniques in the Per-Wer Sanctuary.</u>

Thank you to Dr. Noha Mohamed Hafez for his article on Seshat: "The Scenes of Sefkhet-Abwy at The Temples". *Journal of Association of Arab Universities for Tourism and Hospitality*, 21, 1, 2021, 1-24. doi: 10.21608/jaauth.2021.84216.1200

Thank you to Dr. Jessica Levai for her excellent dissertation *Aspects of the Goddess Nephthys, Especially During the Greco-Roman Period in Egypt.*

Thank you to Asethetepwi and Sesaiaset. Thank you to Maautseshat and Zat.

Thank you to A. Auset Rohn and Rev. Normandi Ellis.

Thank you to Dr. Edward P. Butler.

Thank you to my family and friends. To Mom, Jeremy, Ami, and Dad, who championed education, the sciences, libraries, books, and mathematics.

Thank you to all the librarians who helped me gather sources of information for this book. Thank you to all the Egyptologists for their information on Seshat.

Who is Seshat?

Seshat (Seshet; Seschat)

Seshat is the ancient Egyptian patron goddess of writing, reading, books, architecture, mathematics, astrology, astronomy, recordkeeping, accounting, measurement, time, building temples, building graves, construction, wisdom, knowledge, education, the sciences, magic, and libraries.

Her name can be spelled different ways and pronounced differently. Here are two of the most common variations:

- Seshat (Seh SHOT)
- Seshet (Seh Sheht)[1]

Seshat is a goddess of fate. She is the patron of the "stretching of the cord" ritual that was done before temples were built. She is often depicted as a woman wearing a panther-skin dress, holding a stylus and a reed pen. The spots of the panther represent stars and the night sky; this association makes Seshat the goddess of time, astronomy, and the dead. Her head is adorned with a seven-pointed star with two horns pointed downward. The two horns used to be thought to be a crescent moon.

The meaning of Seshat's name is uncertain, but possible translations are: "Writer"; "Scribe"; "She Who Determines the Lifetime"; "One Who Fixes Fate"; or "She Who is the Scribe".[2] Because

---

[1] Thank you to Rev. Dr. Tamara L. Siuda and Rev. Normandi Ellis and A. Auset Rohn for their guidance on how to pronounce Seshat and Seshet, respectively.

[2] Altenmüller, Hartwig. "Seschat,'die den Leichnam versorgt', als Herrin über Vergangenheit und Geschichte." In Z. Hawass, P. Der Manuelian, R. B. Hussein (Hg.), *Perspectives on Ancient Egypt. Studies in Honor of Edward Brovarski*, Supplément aux Annales du Service des Antiquités de l'Egypte 40, Kairo 2010, S.: 35-37. Hafez, Noha Mohamed. "The Scenes of

of her association with the panther-skin, and one scholar reading the word *wnb* for the rosette as *ndjt* "panther-cat" in the Pyramid Texts, another interpretation of Seshat's name is "Panther Goddess".[3] Yet another interpretation for Seshat's name is based on her association with the deceased. "Seshat was an ancient deity whose job consisted in caring for the body of the deceased and preparing it for burial in the grave."[4] So then her name could mean "One Who Cares for the Corpse".[5]

Hieroglyph for Seshat

The seven-pointed star with the semicircle and two poles on Her head could be a depiction of an instrument used during the "Stretching of the Cord Ritual" at the beginning of building a temple and aligning it to the constellations and the four corners.[6]

Dr. Edward Butler states that the emblem of Seshat is "consisting of a pair of downward pointing bovine horns, enclosing a palmette with seven leaves which may represent a scribe's brush". This emblem may be

---

Sefkhet-Abwy at The Temples". *Journal of Association of Arab Universities for Tourism and Hospitality*, 21, 1, 2021, 1.

[3] Altenmüller, Hartwig. "Seschat, 'die den Leichnam versorgt', als Herrin über Vergangenheit und Geschichte." In Z. Hawass, P. Der Manuelian, R. B. Hussein (Hg.), *Perspectives on Ancient Egypt. Studies in Honor of Edward Brovarski*, Supplément aux Annales du Service des Antiquités de l'Egypte 40, Kairo 2010, S.: 37.

[4] Altenmüller, Hartwig. "Seschat, 'die den Leichnam versorgt', als Herrin über Vergangenheit und Geschichte." In Z. Hawass, P. Der Manuelian, R. B. Hussein (Hg.), *Perspectives on Ancient Egypt. Studies in Honor of Edward Brovarski*, Supplément aux Annales du Service des Antiquités de l'Egypte 40, Kairo 2010, S.: 37.

[5] Altenmüller, Hartwig. "Seschat, 'die den Leichnam versorgt', als Herrin über Vergangenheit und Geschichte." In Z. Hawass, P. Der Manuelian, R. B. Hussein (Hg.), *Perspectives on Ancient Egypt. Studies in Honor of Edward Brovarski*, Supplément aux Annales du Service des Antiquités de l'Egypte 40, Kairo 2010, S.: 37.

[6] Belmonte, Juan Antonio, Miguel Ángel Molinero Polo, and Noemi Miranda. "Unveiling Seshat: New insights into the stretching of the cord ceremony." *In Search of Cosmic Order: Selected Essays on Egyptian Archaeoastronomy* (2009): 207.

where Seshat gets her by-name of *Sefkhet Abwy* "Sevenfold of the Two Horns" or *Sekhef Abwy*, "She Who Releases the Two Horns".[7]

Names of Seshat

Seshat comes in three forms: Seshat, the Great; Seshat, the Small and Sefkhet Abwy. Dagmar Budde, the author of *Die Gottin Seschat*, writes that these three forms of Seshat are categorized thusly:

Seshat the Great
- Great of Magic
- First of Builders
- First of the Library
- Lady of Writing
- Princess of the Library
- Princess of Writing

Seshat, the Small
- First of the Library
- Princess of the Library

Seshat as Sefkhet Abwy
- First of Builders
- First of the Library
- Lady of Writing
- Princess of the Library
- Princess of Writing.[8]

Other names of Seshat include:
- First of the House of Ritual Rules
- Princess of the House of Books (Library)

[7] Butler, Edward. Goddesses and Gods of the Ancient Egyptians: A Theological Encyclopedia: Kindle Edition. (Phaidra Editions, 2021), 277.
[8] Budde, Dagmar. *Die Göttin Seschat*. (H. Wodtke & K. Stegbauer, 2000), 25.

- Lady of Builders[9]

Two ancient theophoric names of people are:
- Ndm-Seshat (Seshat is Pleasant)
- Jm3-Seshat (Seshat is Friendly)[10]

These names may reflect how the ancient people viewed their goddess Seshat as both pleasant and friendly in temperament.

Seshat, Goddess of Writing, Books and Libraries

Seshat is the inventor of writing and recordkeeping.[11] She not only invented writing, but she is also the "Female Creator" and the one "Who Created" writing.

> Seshat, the Female Creator
> Who created writing
> Lady of Writing
> Female Ruler of Scrolls.[12]

Seshat is the patroness of books, writing and libraries. She is called:

- Female Ruler of Papyrus Books[13]
- Lady of the Entire Library[14]

---

[9] Budde, Dagmar. *Die Göttin Seschat*. (H. Wodtke & K. Stegbauer, 2000), 24.

[10] Budde, Dagmar. *Die Göttin Seschat*. (H. Wodtke & K. Stegbauer, 2000), 81.

[11] Butler, Edward. Goddesses and Gods of the Ancient Egyptians: A Theological Encyclopedia: Kindle Edition. (Phaidra Editions, 2021), 277.

[12] Adapted from a translation by Barbara A. Richter in Richter, Barbara A., The Theology of Hathor of Dendera: Aural and Visual Scribal Techniques in the Per-Wer Sanctuary, (Lockwood Press, 2016), 261. Translated by Barbara A. Richter. Used with permission.

[13] Adapted from a translation by Barbara A. Richter in Richter, Barbara A., The Theology of Hathor of Dendera: Aural and Visual Scribal Techniques in the Per-Wer Sanctuary, (Lockwood Press, 2016), 341. Translated by Barbara A. Richter. Used with permission.

- Lady of Library[15]
- Lady of Writing[16]
- Mistress of Writing[17]
- One Who Provides the Texts[18]
- Princess of the Library[19]
- Ruler of the Books[20]
- Sovereign of the House of Books[21]
- Who Created Writing[22]
- Who Makes the Writing of the Books[23]
- Who Resides in the House of the Archivists[24]

---

[14] El-Saghir, Mohamed and Dominique Valbelle. "Komir. I. - The Discovery of Komir Temple. Preliminary Report. II. - Deux hymnes aux divinites de Komir : Anoukis et Nephthys." *BIFAO 83* (1983), p. 164-166.

[15] Hafez, Noha Mohamed. "The Scenes of Sefkhet-Abwy at The Temples". *Journal of Association of Arab Universities for Tourism and Hospitality*, 21, 1, 2021, 7.

[16] Kockelmann, Holger and Erich Winter, *Philae III: Die Zweite Ostkolonnade des Tempels der Isis in Philae. (CO II und CO II K)*, (Verlag der Osterreichischen Akademie der Wissenschaften/Austrian Academy of Sciences, 2016), 141. Translated by Chelsea Bolton.

[17] El-Saghir, Mohamed and Dominique Valbelle. "Komir. I. - The Discovery of Komir Temple. Preliminary Report. II. - Deux hymnes aux divinites de Komir : Anoukis et Nephthys." *BIFAO 83* (1983), p. 164-166.

[18] Kockelmann, Holger and Erich Winter, *Philae III: Die Zweite Ostkolonnade des Tempels der Isis in Philae. (CO II und CO II K)*, (Verlag der Osterreichischen Akademie der Wissenschaften/Austrian Academy of Sciences, 2016), 141. Translated by Chelsea Bolton.

[19] Kockelmann, Holger and Erich Winter, *Philae III: Die Zweite Ostkolonnade des Tempels der Isis in Philae. (CO II und CO II K)*, (Verlag der Osterreichischen Akademie der Wissenschaften/Austrian Academy of Sciences, 2016), 141. Translated by Chelsea Bolton.

[20] Budde, Dagmar. *Die Göttin Seschat.* (H. Wodtke & K. Stegbauer, 2000), 27.

[21] De Wit, Constant. *Les Inscriptions du Temple d'Opet a Karnak III: Traduction integrale des textes rituels-Essai d'interpretation.* (Bruxelles : Edition de la Fondation Egyptologique Reine Elisabeth, 1968), 88.

[22] Adapted from a translation by Barbara A. Richter in Richter, Barbara A., The Theology of Hathor of Dendera: Aural and Visual Scribal Techniques in the Per-Wer Sanctuary, (Lockwood Press, 2016), 261. Translated by Barbara A. Richter. Used with permission.

[23] Budde, Dagmar. *Die Göttin Seschat.* (H. Wodtke & K. Stegbauer, 2000), 73.

[24] El-Saghir, Mohamed and Dominique Valbelle. "Komir. I. - The Discovery of Komir Temple. Preliminary Report. II. - Deux hymnes aux divinites de Komir : Anoukis et Nephthys." *BIFAO 83* (1983), p. 164-166.

Seshat and Temple Building

She is the patroness of the "Stretching of the Cord" ritual done for temples. She outlines the perimeter of the foundation of temples. She is the goddess of the place where rituals are performed and that rituals are done according to the instructions laid out in the sacred texts.[25]

Seshat and Fate

Seshat writes the names of Kings on the Persea Tree, records the royal names and titles of Kings, oversees the coronations, and records the King's lifespan on a palm frond.[26] Djehuty and Seshat write the fate of the child on the birth bricks after the child is born from their mother.[27] Seshat is a goddess of fate because fate is connected to writing and recordkeeping.[28] Seshat also writes the names and deeds of gods, goddesses and humans on the leaves of the Persea Tree (the World Tree in Egyptian mythology). This tree connects the three realms: Sky/Heavens, Earth, and the Underworld. Seshat records all of history on these leaves. She is called the "Keeper of Memories".[29]

Seshat and the Dead

Seshat opens the gateway to the Underworld for the dead.[30] The goddess Seshat also builds buildings for the deceased in the afterlife.[31]

---

[25] Butler, Edward. Goddesses and Gods of the Ancient Egyptians: A Theological Encyclopedia: Kindle Edition. (Phaidra Editions, 2021), 277.

[26] Butler, Edward. Goddesses and Gods of the Ancient Egyptians: A Theological Encyclopedia: Kindle Edition. (Phaidra Editions, 2021), 277.

[27] Pinch, Geraldine. Egyptian Mythology: A Guide to the Gods, Goddesses and Traditions of Ancient Egypt. (New York: Oxford University Press, 2004), 210.

[28] Butler, Edward. Goddesses and Gods of the Ancient Egyptians: A Theological Encyclopedia: Kindle Edition. (Phaidra Editions, 2021), 277.

[29] Hafez, Noha Mohamed. "The Scenes of Sefkhet-Abwy at The Temples". *Journal of Association of Arab Universities for Tourism and Hospitality*, 21, 1, 2021, 1.

[30] Butler, Edward. Goddesses and Gods of the Ancient Egyptians: A Theological Encyclopedia: Kindle Edition. (Phaidra Editions, 2021), 278. In Coffin Texts Spell 10.

[31] Butler, Edward. Goddesses and Gods of the Ancient Egyptians: A Theological Encyclopedia: Kindle Edition. (Phaidra Editions, 2021), 278.

Seshat and Djehuty bring writings to the deceased in the afterlife. Seshat opens the "tomb" and brings the writings to the dead.[32]

Seshat and Music

In the Coffin Text Spell 746, Ihy and Seshat are paired together as ones who can help make music. Ihy is the god of music and the son of the goddess of music, Hethert. They are paired for the creation of both music and lyrics. "My hands are those of Seshat, who is in my mouth as Ihy".[33] Seshat here would be the goddess of writing song lyrics while Ihy is the god of the music itself.

Seshat, Companion of Djehuty (Thoth)

She is often the daughter or sister of Djehuty (Thoth). Djehuty is the ibis headed god of writing, the sciences, knowledge, magic, time, learning, bookkeeping, and the moon. Djehuty and Seshat have much in common. They are both deities of writing, learning, knowledge, education, the sciences, magic, recordkeeping, books, scribes, and libraries. Seshat can be called the "Female Djehuty".[34] They share many epithets such as Lady or Lord of Hermopolis, First of Heseret (Necropolis of Hermopolis Magna) and Lady or Lord of Writing.[35] Seshat is described as one "Who is at the Side of Him Who Knows Egypt (Djehuty)".[36]

According to Richard Wilkinson, Seshat is the daughter, sister, or wife of Djehuty.[37]

---

[32] Butler, Edward. Goddesses and Gods of the Ancient Egyptians: A Theological Encyclopedia: Kindle Edition. (Phaidra Editions, 2021), 278. In Coffin Texts Spell 849.

[33] Butler, Edward. Goddesses and Gods of the Ancient Egyptians: A Theological Encyclopedia: Kindle Edition. (Phaidra Editions, 2021), 278. In Coffin Texts Spell 746.

[34] Budde, Dagmar. *Die Göttin Seschat*. (H. Wodtke & K. Stegbauer, 2000), 149.

[35] Budde, Dagmar. *Die Göttin Seschat*. (H. Wodtke & K. Stegbauer, 2000), 144.

[36] Budde, Dagmar. *Die Göttin Seschat*. (H. Wodtke & K. Stegbauer, 2000), 166.

[37] Wilkinson, Richard H. The Complete Gods and Goddesses of Ancient Egypt. (London: Thames and Hudson, 2003), 166-167.

According to Dagmar Budde, there is some debate whether Seshat is the daughter of Djehuty. It is possible that Seshat as the "Daughter of Djehuty" is due to a mistranslation from the Temple of Dendera.[38] There is another inscription calling Seshat the "Daughter of Djehuty", but this is problematic. Seshat is named in this text rather than Aset, but Aset's image is next to the text. This text could be interpreted as being for the syncretic goddess, Seshat-Aset or Aset-Seshat.[39] Here is the text:

Primordial

Who Began Engraving

Seshat, the Great

With Excellent Magic

Princess

Daughter of Geb

Vizir

Daughter of Djehuty

Who Fills the Palace with Perfection

Who Does What is Right Around the Great Seat (Dendera)

Mother of God.[40]

Instead of his daughter, Seshat is the sister of Djehuty. There is one inscription which describes Seshat as the "Excellent Sister of the Great of Magic (Djehuty)" and another translation in which this passage is not about Djehuty, but about Seshat Herself. "Excellent Sister as the Great of Magic".[41] Seshat is called the "Sister of Djehuty" in another inscription.[42]

There are some inscriptions with these two deities:

---

[38] Budde, Dagmar. _Die Göttin Seschat_. (H. Wodtke & K. Stegbauer, 2000), 145.

[39] Budde, Dagmar. _Die Göttin Seschat_. (H. Wodtke & K. Stegbauer, 2000), 146.

[40] Budde, Dagmar. _Die Göttin Seschat_. (H. Wodtke & K. Stegbauer, 2000), 146.

[41] Budde, Dagmar. _Die Göttin Seschat_. (H. Wodtke & K. Stegbauer, 2000), 145. Footnote 17.

[42] Budde, Dagmar. _Die Göttin Seschat_. (H. Wodtke & K. Stegbauer, 2000), 145.

Djehuty, the Lord of the Words of God
and Seshat, Who Makes the Writing of the Books.[43]

Djehuty, Lord of Hermopolis and
Seshat, Mistress of Writing.[44]

Seshat is mentioned in the *Book of Thoth*, a book written in Demotic. Seshat is called Sheit (Shait) meaning "Primeval One". The word Shait here does not mean the god Shai or the word fate. Within the text, Seshat is associated with the "Chamber of Darkness".[45] The "Chamber of Darkness" is a place the initiate goes to during a ritual and is said "to bark among the dogs of Sheit [Seshat], the Great" (B07, 17).[46] Edward Butler then describes a Greek text called, "Dialogues of Dogs" (translated to Greek by Eudoxus; Diogenes Laertius 8.89). The text calls Seshat both a "Huntress" and a "Trapper" (C04.1, 12-13).[47] At Hermopolis, at the Temple of Djehuty, Seshat was associated with the "House of the Fishnet".[48]

One who is a scribe is described as "whom Djehuty Himself has taught, into whose mouth Seshat has spat". This resembles a Greek myth recorded by Apollodorus where Polyeidos taught Glaukos the arts. Polyeidos then had Glaukos spit into Polyeidos's mouth so that the knowledge of the arts would leave Glaukos.[49]

[43] Budde, Dagmar. *Die Göttin Seschat*. (H. Wodtke & K. Stegbauer, 2000), 73.
[44] Budde, Dagmar. *Die Göttin Seschat*. (H. Wodtke & K. Stegbauer, 2000), 73.
[45] Butler, Edward. Goddesses and Gods of the Ancient Egyptians: A Theological Encyclopedia: Kindle Edition. (Phaidra Editions, 2021), 278.
[46] Butler, Edward. Goddesses and Gods of the Ancient Egyptians: A Theological Encyclopedia: Kindle Edition. (Phaidra Editions, 2021), 278.
[47] Butler, Edward. Goddesses and Gods of the Ancient Egyptians: A Theological Encyclopedia: Kindle Edition. (Phaidra Editions, 2021), 278.
[48] Butler, Edward. Goddesses and Gods of the Ancient Egyptians: A Theological Encyclopedia: Kindle Edition. (Phaidra Editions, 2021), 278.
[49] Butler, Edward. Goddesses and Gods of the Ancient Egyptians: A Theological Encyclopedia: Kindle Edition. (Phaidra Editions, 2021), 279.

Seshat and Her Sister Mafdet

The goddess Mafdet is a serval, cheetah or leopard headed goddess who is over war, protection, and execution of enemies. She can also be depicted as a mongoose.

Seshat and Mafdet are also associated with the panther, the panther skin of mortuary priests and the golden color of the panther skin in their shared epithet, "Gold".[50] Like Nebet Het and Aset, Seshat and Mafdet are called, "Twin Sisters". Mafdet and Seshat share a birthday.[51]

Seshat and Harpokrates and Wesir (Osiris)

Heru-pa-Khered or Harpocrates or Harpokrates is the child form of Heru (Horus). Harpokrates is the son of Seshat in this inscription, "Who Grants Her Son Harpokrates Numerous Years".[52] So, Seshat is the Mother of Heru, the Child.

In the Coffin Texts, Seshat is furious at a child she bore.[53]

In the *Papyrus of Tebtunis*, Seshat is called the "Daughter of Wesir".[54]

Sefkhet Abwy
Lady of Writing
Princess of the House of Books
Daughter of Wesir
Who Has Lost Her Reunited Father.[55]

---

[50] Westendorf, Wolfhart. "Beiträge aus und zu den medizinischen Texten." *Zeitschrift für ägyptische Sprache und Altertumskunde* 92, no. 1 (1966): 137-139.

[51] Westendorf, Wolfhart. "Beiträge aus und zu den medizinischen Texten." *Zeitschrift für ägyptische Sprache und Altertumskunde* 92, no. 1 (1966): 136.

[52] Budde, Dagmar. <u>Die Göttin Seschat</u>. (H. Wodtke & K. Stegbauer, 2000), 155.

[53] Pinch, Geraldine. <u>Egyptian Mythology: A Guide to the Gods, Goddesses and Traditions of Ancient Egypt</u>. (New York: Oxford University Press, 2004), 190.

[54] Budde, Dagmar. <u>Die Göttin Seschat</u>. (H. Wodtke & K. Stegbauer, 2000), 177.

[55] Budde, Dagmar. <u>Die Göttin Seschat</u>. (H. Wodtke & K. Stegbauer, 2000), 177-178.

Seshat and Her Animals

Seshat is heavily associated with the leopard since she wears a leopard print dress and the spots of the animal symbolize the souls of the dead.

Within the *Book of Thoth*, Seshat is associated with dogs. According to Edward Butler, Seshat is associated with dogs possibly because she is a huntress in this text.[56] Within the *Book of Thoth*, Seshat is called Shait (Primeval One) and the text reads, "wish to bark among the dogs of Shait [Seshat], the great".[57] Dogs are also likened to scribes in another text, "dogs which are as scribes."[58]

Seshat is called, "She Who is Wise, this one who first established the chamber, she being a lamp of prophecy."[59] Seshat is a wise goddess, one who created the Chamber of Darkness and who is a prophetess.[60]

Seshat and Other Goddesses

Seshat has many syncretisms with other ancient Egyptian Goddesses, including Nebet Het, Aset, Nit, Hethert, and Raettawy. Seshat is also identified with Ma'at, Mut, Sopdet (Sirius) and Tefnut.[61]

Egyptologist Dr. Tamara L. Siuda notes that Seshat is heavily associated with Nit (Neith) and Nebet Het (Nepththys). In her book, *Nebt-Het, Lady of the House*, Siuda gives evidence for connections

---

[56] Butler, Edward P. "Opening the Way of Writing: Semiotic Metaphysics in the Book of Thoth." In *Practicing Gnosis*, (Brill, 2013), pp. 248.

[57] Butler, Edward P. "Opening the Way of Writing: Semiotic Metaphysics in the Book of Thoth." In *Practicing Gnosis*, (Brill, 2013), pp. 248.

[58] Butler, Edward P. "Opening the Way of Writing: Semiotic Metaphysics in the Book of Thoth." In *Practicing Gnosis*, (Brill, 2013), pp. 248.

[59] Butler, Edward P. "Opening the Way of Writing: Semiotic Metaphysics in the Book of Thoth." In *Practicing Gnosis*, (Brill, 2013), pp. 251.

[60] Butler, Edward P. "Opening the Way of Writing: Semiotic Metaphysics in the Book of Thoth." In *Practicing Gnosis*, (Brill, 2013), pp. 251-252.

[61] Pereira, Ronaldo Guilherme Gurgel. "Some Remarks on the Book of Thoth: concerning Seshat, Shai and the 'invention'of the Hermetic Agathos Daimon." In *International Congress for Young Egyptologists*, vol. 25, 2012, 49 and 50. Belmonte, Juan Antonio, Miguel Ángel Molinero Polo, and Noemi Miranda. "Unveiling Seshat: New insights into the stretching of the cord ceremony." *In Search of Cosmic Order: Selected Essays on Egyptian Archaeoastronomy* (2009): 204. Sauneron, Serge, *Esna V: Les fêtes religieuses d'Esna aux derniers siècles du paganisme*, (Cairo: IFAO, 1962; 2004), 289-291.

between these three goddesses,[62] one of which is that these goddesses were connected in the texts of the Temple of Esna.[63]

A syncretic deity are two or more deities that merge to form a single entity. So, Seshat, Aset, and Seshat-Aset are three separate goddesses. Sometimes in hymns, names of other gods are used as titles of other gods, so sometimes the line is blurred if it is a syncretism or a title of a deity unless it is explicitly stated.

Seshat and Nebet Het (Nephthys)

Nebet Het and Seshat are connected to each other as two aspects of the same goddess, a syncretism of two goddesses or as titles of each other.

The emblem of Seshat is her name in hieroglyphs and sits on top of Seshat's head. This sign is a rosette (7-pointed emblem) on a stem with an upturned half-circle on her head. According to Altenmuller, the rosette could be a flower, horns or a sign for royal authority or an early form of the word for deity. The rod with the 7-pointed emblem could be an early form of the word for "God or Goddess" and the semicircle above the rod could be the roof. So, this emblem could mean "Hall or House of God". This can also function as a logogram, meaning "Who supplied the corpse." The double ostrich feather over the semicircle could denote holiness or sacredness of the space. So, the emblem of Seshat could denote a sacred space or building of which Seshat is its Mistress. This word for house could also be the House of Embalming. This mirrors Nebet Het's name which means "Lady of the House/Temple/Tomb". So, both Nebet Het's name and Seshat's emblem can be "Lady of the House/Temple/Tomb". According to Altenmuller, Seshat is an "older name for Nebet Het (Nephthys)".[64]

---

[62] Siuda, Tamara L. Nebt Het: Lady of the House. (2010), 8-11.
[63] Siuda, Tamara L. Nebt Het: Lady of the House. (2010), 11.
[64] Altenmüller, Hartwig. "Seschat,'die den Leichnam versorgt', als Herrin über Vergangenheit und Geschichte." In Z. Hawass, P. Der Manuelian, R. B. Hussein (Hg.), *Perspectives on Ancient Egypt. Studies in Honor of Edward Brovarski*, Supplément aux Annales du Service des Antiquités de l'Egypte 40, Kairo 2010, S.: 42-44.

Within both the Pyramid and Coffin Texts, Nebet Het is identified with Seshat as Nebet Het-Seshat: "Nebet Het has collected all your members for you in her name of Seshat, Lady of Builders."[65] According to Siuda, this passage from the Pyramid Texts "blatantly" mentions Seshat as a form of Nebet Het.[66] And in the Coffin Texts, again:

(O Name of Deceased Person)
Heru protects you
He causes Nebet Het to hold you together
To create you in Her Name of Seshat, Mistress of Potters
She is a Great Lady, Great of Life in the Night-boat
Who raises Heru up.[67]

Seshat's connection to Nebet Het is alluded to in this inscription from the Temple of Behbeit el Hagar from the Ptolemaic Period. "Seshat, the Great One, Who Protects Her Brother Wesir in *Per-Ka* and his limbs united".[68] Seshat is called the one "Who Protects Her Brother Wesir" which is normally Nebet Het's role as a guardian and sister of Wesir. Nebet Het and Seshat are both protecting and caring for the deceased and Wesir. Nebet Het as Seshat here is the "Mistress of Builders" whose role is to build graves for the dead. In Coffin Texts 355, the deceased says: "Seshat built my house for me" and in another inscription, it says: "in that house that Seshat built for me". The "house" here is the tomb or grave of the deceased.[69] Nebet Het and

---

[65] Siuda, Tamara L. Nebt Het: Lady of the House. (2010), 14; and Faulkner, R.O. The Ancient Egyptian Pyramid Texts, 119. Pyramid Text 364.

[66] Siuda, Tamara L. Nebt Het: Lady of the House. (2010), 14; Wainwright, Gerald A. "Seshat and the Pharaoh," 30, 33, and 39.

[67] Translation by Siuda, Tamara L. in The Ancient Egyptian Prayerbook. (Stargazer Design, 2009), 73.

[68] Altenmüller, Hartwig. "Seschat,'die den Leichnam versorgt', als Herrin über Vergangenheit und Geschichte." In Z. Hawass, P. Der Manuelian, R. B. Hussein (Hg.), *Perspectives on Ancient Egypt. Studies in Honor of Edward Brovarski*, Supplément aux Annales du Service des Antiquités de l'Egypte 40, Kairo 2010, S.: 38.

[69] Altenmüller, Hartwig. "Seschat,'die den Leichnam versorgt', als Herrin über Vergangenheit und Geschichte." In Z. Hawass, P. Der Manuelian, R. B. Hussein (Hg.), *Perspectives on*

Seshat are associated with reuniting the limbs of the dead and embalming the deceased. Seshat as the Mistress of Architecture would also be the one who restores the dead and builds their graves. These are traits that Nebet Het shares with Seshat. Nebet Het and Seshat are showing their funerary aspects here.[70]

Nebet Het and Seshat are both caretakers of Heru-sa-Aset. "Aset is his Mother. Nebet Het is his nurse. Seshat is She of Heru. She is the one who fed him".[71]

Nebet Het is given titles associated with books, pottery, and builders. These are "Lady of Books," "Lady of Builders," and "Mistress of Potters."[72] Nebet Het and Seshat share other epithets and functions such as "Lady of the Library" and "Lady of Writing."[73] Nebet Het is also called Seshat in an inscription which includes associations with writing and temples:

Nebet Het, Sister of God
Seshat, the Great
Mistress of Writing
Who Controls the Temples.[74]

Ancient Egypt. Studies in Honor of Edward Brovarski, Supplément aux Annales du Service des Antiquités de l'Egypte 40, Kairo 2010, S.: 38-39.

[70] Altenmüller, Hartwig. "Seschat,'die den Leichnam versorgt', als Herrin über Vergangenheit und Geschichte." In Z. Hawass, P. Der Manuelian, R. B. Hussein (Hg.), *Perspectives on Ancient Egypt. Studies in Honor of Edward Brovarski*, Supplément aux Annales du Service des Antiquités de l'Egypte 40, Kairo 2010, S.: 37-39.

[71] Dunand, Francoise. Le Culte D'Isis Et Les Ptolémées. (Netherlands: Brill, 2015), 8.

[72] Faulkner, R.O. The Ancient Egyptian Pyramid Texts, 119. Pyramid Text 364; and Siuda, Tamara L. Nebt Het: Lady of the House. (2010), 14; and Faulkner, R.O. The Ancient Egyptian Coffin Texts Vol 1-3. Translated by R.O. Faulkner. (England: Aris & Phillips, Ltd., 2004), 304. Coffin Text 778.

[73] Leitz, Christian, and Dagmar Budde, et. al. Lexikon der Ägyptischen Götter und Götterbezeichnungen (LGG, OLA 129, Band 8). (Peeters, 2003), 286; and Siuda, Tamara L. Nebt Het: Lady of the House. (2010), 30.

[74] De Wit, Constant. *Les Inscriptions du Temple d'Opet a Karnak III: Traduction integrale des textes rituels-Essai d'interpretation.* (Bruxelles : Edition de la Fondation Egyptologique Reine Elisabeth, 1968), 80.

Both Seshat and Nebet Het were associated with beauty. Seshat was the patroness of "cosmetics and beauty".[75] Nebet Het and Seshat both share the title *Kherseket* (She Who Wipes Away Tears).[76] Seshat is called the "August *Kherseket*" in a temple inscription.[77] *Kherseket* is a common title for Nebet Het. Seshat and Nebet Het share another title, *Merkhetes* (She Whose Flame is Painful).[78] According to Edward Butler, *Shentait* (Aset, the Widow) and *Merkhetes* (Nebet Het) appear together in the Letopolitan Rite. Within the Demotic *Book of Thoth*, *Shentait* (Aset) appears with *Merkhetes* again, but *Merkhetes* here is Seshat instead of Nebet Het.[79]

In the Hymn of Nebet Het from the Temple of Komir, Nebet Het is called the names of many Goddesses including Seshat.

To You, Seshat the Great, Mistress of Men
Mistress of Writing, Lady of the Entire Library
To You,
Who commands the divine decrees
Great of Magic
Who resides in the House of the Archivists.[80]

Nebet Het was even identified with different aspects of Seshat, such as Seshat, Seshat the Great, and the Small Seshat.[81]

---

[75] Levai, Jessica. Aspects of the Goddess Nephthys, 170-171.

[76] El-Tonssy, Mohamed A. "The Goddess Rattawy in Greco-Roman Temples." In *The Fifteen Conference Book of the General of Arab Archaeologists*, (2012-2013), pp. 199. I changed the spelling of "Khereseket" to "Kherseket".

[77] El-Tonssy, Mohamed A. "The Goddess Rattawy in Greco-Roman Temples." In *The Fifteen Conference Book of the General of Arab Archaeologists*, (2012-2013), pp. 199. I changed the spelling of "Khereseket" to "Kherseket".

[78] Butler, Edward P. "Opening the Way of Writing: Semiotic Metaphysics in the Book of Thoth." In *Practicing Gnosis*, (Brill, 2013), pp. 229.

[79] Butler, Edward P. "Opening the Way of Writing: Semiotic Metaphysics in the Book of Thoth." In *Practicing Gnosis*, (Brill, 2013), pp. 229.

[80] El-Saghir, Mohamed and Dominique Valbelle. "Komir. I. - The Discovery of Komir Temple. Preliminary Report. II. - Deux hymnes aux divinites de Komir : Anoukis et Nephthys." *BIFAO 83* (1983), p. 164-166.

[81] Leitz, Christian, and Dagmar Budde, et. Al Lexikon der Ägyptischen Götter und Götterbezeichnunge

Nebet Het
With the Excellent Heart
Small Seshat
Princess of the House of Life.[82]

There is also a syncretic deity Nebet Het-Seshat. Both Seshat and Nebet Het share the sacred animals of the dog and the leopard/panther.[83]

Seshat and Nit (Neith)

In a text, Seshat is called a "Huntress" and at the Temple of Hermopolis, catches fish in a net.[84] Nit is the goddess of hunting. In a hymn to Nit, Nit is identified with Seshat:

Seshat, the Great
Mistress of Writing.[85]

Seshat and Anuket (Anukis)

In one hymn, Seshat and Anuket are connected. Anuket is the goddess of the cataracts of the Nile, fertility, and protection as an Eye of Ra. Her sacred animal was the gazelle.

(LGG, OLA 129, Band 8). (Peeters, 2003), 292.

[82] Budde, Dagmar. _Die Göttin Seschat_. (H. Wodtke & K. Stegbauer, 2000), 216.

[83] Leitz, Christian, and Dagmar Budde, et. al. Lexikon der Ägyptischen Götter und Götterbezeichnungen (LGG, OLA 129, Band 8). (Peeters, 2003), 287. Altenmüller, Hartwig. "Seschat,'die den Leichnam versorgt', als Herrin über Vergangenheit und Geschichte." In Z. Hawass, P. Der Manuelian, R. B. Hussein (Hg.), _Perspectives on Ancient Egypt. Studies in Honor of Edward Brovarski_, Supplément aux Annales du Service des Antiquités de l'Egypte 40, Kairo 2010, S.: 37. Butler, Edward P. "Opening the Way of Writing: Semiotic Metaphysics in the Book of Thoth." In _Practicing Gnosis_, (Brill, 2013), pp. 248.

[84] Butler, Edward. Goddesses and Gods of the Ancient Egyptians: A Theological Encyclopedia: Kindle Edition. (Phaidra Editions, 2021), 278.

[85] Sauneron, Serge, _Esna V: Les fêtes religieuses d'Esna aux derniers siècles du paganisme_, (Cairo: IFAO, 1962; 2004), 289-291.

Anuket (Anukis)
Lady of Elephantine
First of Philae
Who Stays in Bigge
Seshat, the Great
Lady of Writing in the House of Books
Great of Magic
Eye of Ra
Lady of the Sky
and Princess of All the Gods.[86]

Seshat and Sopdet (Sothis; Sirius Star)

Seshat and Sopdet are connected in a text.

Sopdet, Lady of the Stars
Seshat, the Great
Lady of Writing.[87]

Seshat and Hethert (Hathor)

Seshat is called Hethert in a hymn.

The Female King of Upper and Lower Egypt
Seshat, the Primordial One
Who invented writing
Lady of Writing, Female Ruler of Scrolls
Noble and Powerful Lady
Without another except for Her
The *Atenet*, who shines in the sky

---

[86] Budde, Dagmar. *Die Göttin Seschat*. (H. Wodtke & K. Stegbauer, 2000), 152.

[87] Budde, Dagmar. *Die Göttin Seschat*. (H. Wodtke & K. Stegbauer, 2000), 186.

> What goes forth from Her mouth comes into being at once
> Hethert, the Great, Lady of Iunet.[88]

Hethert is called "Seshat, the Great, Mistress of Writing" and "Seshat, the Great, Mistress of the House of Books" in a hymn.[89]

In another hymn, Hethert is called Seshat. Seshat here is given titles describing her as a protector of Wesir, one with the brilliant face and a goddess of the gemstone, turquoise.

> Seshat, the Great
> Who Protects Her Brother Wesir
> One with the Shining Face
> Mistress of Turquoise.[90]

Like Hethert, Seshat is a primordial goddess. Seshat invented writing, she is the female scribe and is the patroness of scrolls and writing. Seshat is associated with the Female Sun Disk (Atenet) and the shining power of the sun.

Seshat and Aset (Auset, Iset; Isis)

Seshat is a title or syncretization with Aset. Here is one hymn which calls Aset the name and titles of Seshat.

> Seshat, the Great,
> Princess of the Library
> Great of Magic
> Princess of All the Gods.[91]

---

[88] Adapted from a translation by Barbara A. Richter in Richter, Barbara A., The Theology of Hathor of Dendera: Aural and Visual Scribal Techniques in the Per-Wer Sanctuary, (Lockwood Press, 2016), 380. Translated by Barbara A. Richter. Used with permission.

[89] Budde, Dagmar. *Die Göttin Seschat*. (H. Wodtke & K. Stegbauer, 2000), 157.

[90] Kurth, Dieter. *Edfou VII*. Vol. 1-2. (Otto Harrassowitz Verlag, 2004), 499.

[91] Kockelmann, Holger and Erich Winter, *Philae III: Die Zweite Ostkolonnade des Tempels der Isis in Philae. (CO II und CO II K)*, (Verlag der Osterreichischen Akademie der

There are many ancient hymns in which Aset is called by the name Seshat with her titles.[92] One hymn is:

Aset, the Great
Mother of God
Lady of the Temple of Aset
Lady of the Gods
First of Dendera
Seshat, the Great
Princess of Writing
Great of Magic
Lady of the House of Books
Great in the Sky, Powerful on Earth
For Whom the Gods Rise to Worship
Daily.[93]

Here is another one:

Aset Pechat
Mistress of Writing
Great Seshat
Princess of the House of Books.[94]

Like Aset, Seshat is a great magician, a female librarian, and a member of the royal family of gods. Both goddesses have the title of "Great of Magic". Aset is the goddess of magic par excellence, while Seshat is the goddess of the magic inherent in the written word. Both

---

Wissenschaften/Austrian Academy of Sciences, 2016), 143. Translated by Chelsea Bolton. I changed Isis to her ancient Egyptian name Aset.

[92] Budde, Dagmar. *Die Göttin Seschat*. (H. Wodtke & K. Stegbauer, 2000), 163-167.
[93] Budde, Dagmar. *Die Göttin Seschat*. (H. Wodtke & K. Stegbauer, 2000), 165.
[94] Budde, Dagmar. *Die Göttin Seschat*. (H. Wodtke & K. Stegbauer, 2000), 216.

goddesses are associated with education, knowledge, books, writing, and libraries.

There is another inscription which connects Aset-Hededet, Seshat and Djehuty.

Aset Hededet (Luminous One) in dealings
Seshat, the Great
Who is at the Side of Him Who Knows Egypt (Djehuty).[95]

Seshat and Raettawy (Raittawy)

Seshat is the title of Raettawy in this hymn. This can also be interpreted as a syncretism.

Seshat, Mistress of the Library
She Who protects the sun god with Her chosen spells
Wet nurse of Heru by Her spells.[96]

Like Raettawy, Seshat is a protector of the sun god, Ra using magic and a nurse of Heru. Seshat is associated with the library. One text read, "Raettawy-Seshat, is also called there, an Eye of Ra".[97]

Conclusion

Seshat is the Female Scribe, the inventor of writing and the female creator of writing. She is the goddess of writing, learning, knowledge, wisdom, record keeping, mathematics, bookkeeping, architecture, measurement, astronomy, fate, and the building of temples and graves. She is the goddess whose sacred animals are the dog and leopard. Seshat is the patroness of scribes, writers, and librarians. She a prophetess and

---

[95] Budde, Dagmar. _Die Göttin Seschat_. (H. Wodtke & K. Stegbauer, 2000), 166.

[96] Adapted from El-Tonssy, Mohamed A. "The Goddess Rattawy in Greco-Roman Temples." In _The Fifteen Conference Book of the General of Arab Archaeologists_, (2012-2013), pp. 197. I spelled Rattawy as Raettawy. I left out "is the" in the first line. I changed "Mistress of Library" to "Mistress of the Library".

[97] Budde, Dagmar. _Die Göttin Seschat_. (H. Wodtke & K. Stegbauer, 2000), 26.

a guardian of the deceased. Like Nebet Het, Seshat has the title of *Kherseket* (She Who Wipes Away Tears) and *Merkhetes* (She Whose Flame is Painful).

Seshat is the daughter, wife, or sister of Djehuty. Seshat has a twin sister, Mafdet. Seshat is a multifaceted goddess who is a writer, architect, protector, comforter of the grieving, guardian, prophetess, and a recordkeeper of knowledge.

HYMNS OF SESHAT

(Seshet; Sefkhet-abwy)

Hymn of Seshat

Hail to You,
Noble Lady, Female Ruler
Mistress of Goddesses
Seshat, the Great
Lady of Writing.[98]

---

[98] Adapted from a translation by Barbara A. Richter in Richter, Barbara A., The Theology of Hathor of Dendera: Aural and Visual Scribal Techniques in the Per-Wer Sanctuary, (Lockwood Press, 2016), 301. Translated by Barbara A. Richter. Used with permission.

HYMN OF SESHAT

Seshat, the Primordial One
Who initiated writing.[99]

---

[99] Adapted from a translation by Barbara A. Richter in Richter, Barbara A., The Theology of Hathor of Dendera: Aural and Visual Scribal Techniques in the Per-Wer Sanctuary, (Lockwood Press, 2016), 503. Translated by Barbara A. Richter. Used with permission.

Hymn of Seshat

The Female King of Upper and Lower Egypt
Seshat, the Primordial One
Who created writing
Lady of Writing
Female Ruler of Papyrus Books
Noble and Powerful Lady
Without another except for Her
The *Atenet* who shines in the sky
What goes forth from Her mouth comes into being at once
Hethert, the Great, Lady of Iunet.[100]

---

[100] Adapted from a translation by Barbara A. Richter in Richter, Barbara A., The Theology of Hathor of Dendera: Aural and Visual Scribal Techniques in the Per-Wer Sanctuary, (Lockwood Press, 2016), 341. Translated by Barbara A. Richter. Used with permission.

HYMN OF SESHAT

The Female King of Upper and Lower Egypt
Seshat, the Primordial One
Who invented writing
Lady of Writing, Female Ruler of Scrolls
Noble and Powerful Lady
Without another except for Her
The *Atenet*, who shines in the sky
What goes forth from Her mouth comes into being at once
Hethert, the Great, Lady of Iunet.[101]

---

[101] Adapted from a translation by Barbara A. Richter in Richter, Barbara A., The Theology of Hathor of Dendera: Aural and Visual Scribal Techniques in the Per-Wer Sanctuary, (Lockwood Press, 2016), 380. Translated by Barbara A. Richter. Used with permission.

HYMN OF SESHAT

Seshat, the Female Creator
Who created writing
Lady of Writing
Female Ruler of Scrolls.[102]

---

[102] Adapted from a translation by Barbara A. Richter in Richter, Barbara A., *The Theology of Hathor of Dendera: Aural and Visual Scribal Techniques in the Per-Wer Sanctuary*, (Lockwood Press, 2016), 261. Translated by Barbara A. Richter. Used with permission.

HYMN OF SESHAT

Seshat, the Great
Princess of the Library
Lady of Writing
One who provides the texts
Guarded in Her vicinity.[103]

---

[103] Kockelmann, Holger and Erich Winter, *Philae III: Die Zweite Ostkolonnade des Tempels der Isis in Philae. (CO II und CO II K)*, (Verlag der Osterreichischen Akademie der Wissenschaften/Austrian Academy of Sciences, 2016), 141. Translated by Chelsea Bolton.

HYMN OF SESHAT

Seshat, the Great
Lady of Writing
The Great, the Living One
Head of the Library.[104]

---

[104] Translated from Hafez, Noha Mohamed. "The Scenes of Sefkhet-Abwy at The Temples". *Journal of Association of Arab Universities for Tourism and Hospitality*, 21, 1, 2021, 6.

HYMN OF SESHAT

Seshat, the Great
Sefkhet Abwy
Lady of Writing
Mistress of the Library
Overseer of the House.[105]

---

[105] Translated from Hafez, Noha Mohamed. "The Scenes of Sefkhet-Abwy at The Temples". *Journal of Association of Arab Universities for Tourism and Hospitality*, 21, 1, 2021, 7.

HYMN OF SESHAT

Seshat, the Great
Lady of Writing
Sefkhet Abwy
The Overseer
Lady of the Library
The Overseer.[106]

---

[106] Translated from Hafez, Noha Mohamed. "The Scenes of Sefkhet-Abwy at The Temples". *Journal of Association of Arab Universities for Tourism and Hospitality*, 21, 1, 2021, 7.

HYMN OF SESHAT

Seshat, the Great
Head of the Library
Overseer of the House
Lady of Thoth, the Overseer
Who is in the Heart of the Temple of Behdet (Edfu)
Sefkhet, Foremost of the Temple
Protector
Overseer.[107]

---

[107] Translated from Hafez, Noha Mohamed. "The Scenes of Sefkhet-Abwy at The Temples". *Journal of Association of Arab Universities for Tourism and Hospitality*, 21, 1, 2021, 7.

HYMN OF SESHAT

Seshat, the Great
Sefkhet Abwy
Lady of Writing
Foremost of the Library
Overseer of the House.[108]

---

[108] Translated from Hafez, Noha Mohamed. "The Scenes of Sefkhet-Abwy at The Temples". *Journal of Association of Arab Universities for Tourism and Hospitality*, 21, 1, 2021, 7-8.

HYMN OF SESHAT

Seshat, the Great
Sefkhet Abwy
Lady of Writing
Head of the Library
The Overseer.[109]

---

[109] Translated from Hafez, Noha Mohamed. "The Scenes of Sefkhet-Abwy at The Temples". *Journal of Association of Arab Universities for Tourism and Hospitality*, 21, 1, 2021, 8.

HYMN OF SESHAT

Seshat, the Great
Lady of Writing
Sefkhet
Lady of the Library
Overseer of the House.[110]

---

[110] Translated from Hafez, Noha Mohamed. "The Scenes of Sefkhet-Abwy at The Temples". *Journal of Association of Arab Universities for Tourism and Hospitality*, 21, 1, 2021, 8.

HYMN OF SESHAT

Seshat, the Great
Lady of Writing
Sefkhet Abwy
Mistress of the Library
Given many jubilees.[111]

---

[111] Translated from Hafez, Noha Mohamed. "The Scenes of Sefkhet-Abwy at The Temples". *Journal of Association of Arab Universities for Tourism and Hospitality*, 21, 1, 2021, 10.

HYMN OF SESHAT

Seshat, the Great
Mistress of the Library
Overseer of the House
Sefkhet
Lady of Writing.[112]

---

[112] Translated from Hafez, Noha Mohamed. "The Scenes of Sefkhet-Abwy at The Temples". *Journal of Association of Arab Universities for Tourism and Hospitality*, 21, 1, 2021, 10.

HYMN OF SESHAT

Seshat, the Great
Ruler and Mistress of Writing
Sefkhet Abwy
First of the House of Books
Who bestowed the years of the Sed Festival
On the magnificent power being in Dendera
as a Kingdom of Millions upon Millions of Years.[113]

---

[113] Budde, Dagmar. *Die Göttin Seschat*. (H. Wodtke & K. Stegbauer, 2000), 20.

HYMN OF SESHAT

Great Seshat is resplendent in Shenes
and prolongs the Kingship for Her son.
She is Great of Magic
Magnificent in the House of Life
Princess in the House of Ritual Rules.[114]

---

[114] Budde, Dagmar. *Die Göttin Seschat*. (H. Wodtke & K. Stegbauer, 2000), 59.

HYMN OF SESHAT

Seshat, the Great
Mistress of Writing
Princess of the House of Books
Mistress of Years
Who Gives to Whom She Loves.[115]

---

[115] Budde, Dagmar. *Die Göttin Seschat*. (H. Wodtke & K. Stegbauer, 2000), 111.

HYMN OF SESHAT

Seshat, the Great
Mistress of Writing
Great of Magic
Princess of the House of Books.[116]

---

[116] Budde, Dagmar. *Die Göttin Seschat*. (H. Wodtke & K. Stegbauer, 2000), 119.

HYMN OF SESHAT

Seshat, Great
Mistress of Writing
First of the House of Books.[117]

---

[117] Budde, Dagmar. *Die Göttin Seschat*. (H. Wodtke & K. Stegbauer, 2000), 98.

HYMN OF SESHAT

Seshat, Mistress of Writing
Lady of the Sky
Princess of the Gods.[118]

---

[118] Budde, Dagmar. *Die Göttin Seschat*. (H. Wodtke & K. Stegbauer, 2000), 99.

HYMN OF SESHAT

Seshat, the Great
Mistress of Writing
Great of Magic in the House of Books
Who Prolongs the Years of Him Who is on the Throne
The Magnificent and Mighty in Behdet.[119]

---

[119] Budde, Dagmar. *Die Göttin Seschat*. (H. Wodtke & K. Stegbauer, 2000), 120.

HYMN OF SESHAT

Seshat, the Great
Sefkhet Abwy
Mistress of Writing in the House of Books
Mistress of Walking in the Palace
With a wide seat in the House of the Sed Festivals
Primordial
Mistress of What is Written in the House of the Ritual Rules
Perfect Renenutet in the House of Heru (Edfu).[120]

---

[120] Budde, Dagmar. *Die Göttin Seschat*. (H. Wodtke & K. Stegbauer, 2000), 120.

HYMN OF SESHAT

Seshat, the Great
Mistress of Writing
Who Calculates All Things.[121]

---

[121] Budde, Dagmar. *Die Göttin Seschat*. (H. Wodtke & K. Stegbauer, 2000), 122.

HYMN OF SESHAT

Seshat, the Great
Sefkhet Abwy
Princess of the House of Books
Who Records the Kingship for the Son of Aset.[122]

---

[122] Budde, Dagmar. *Die Göttin Seschat*. (H. Wodtke & K. Stegbauer, 2000), 123.

HYMN OF SESHAT

Small Seshat
First of the House of Books
Excellent Sister as the Great of Magic.[123]

---

[123] Budde, Dagmar. *Die Göttin Seschat*. (H. Wodtke & K. Stegbauer, 2000), 145. Footnote 17.

Hymn of Seshat

Seshat, the Great
Lady of the House of Books
Sefkhet Abwy
Lady of Writing
Who grants Her son Harpokrates numerous years
Who draws up the ground plant of the House where He was
    born.[124]

---

[124] Budde, Dagmar. *Die Göttin Seschat*. (H. Wodtke & K. Stegbauer, 2000), 155.

HYMN OF SESHAT

Seshat, the Great
With Her Books.[125]

---

[125] Budde, Dagmar. *Die Göttin Seschat*. (H. Wodtke & K. Stegbauer, 2000), 200.

HYMN OF SESHAT

Seshat, the Great
First of the House of Ritual Rules
Mistress of Writing and
Ruler of Books
Primordial
Who Began Engraving Among the Goddesses
Who Gives Orders in the Palace.[126]

---

[126] Budde, Dagmar. *Die Göttin Seschat*. (H. Wodtke & K. Stegbauer, 2000), 201.

HYMN OF SESHAT

Magnificent, Ruler
Princess of the Goddesses
Seshat, the Great
Mistress of Writing...
Seshat, the Great
Mistress of the House of Books.[127]

---

[127] Budde, Dagmar. *Die Göttin Seschat*. (H. Wodtke & K. Stegbauer, 2000), 157.

HYMN OF SESHAT

Seshat, the Primordial
Who Began Writing
Mistress of Writing
Ruler of the Books.[128]

---

[128] Budde, Dagmar. *Die Göttin Seschat*. (H. Wodtke & K. Stegbauer, 2000), 157.

HYMN OF SESHAT

Seshat, the Great
Mistress of Writing
Sefkhet-Abwy
Sovereign of the House of Books
Eye of Ra, Mistress of the Sky.[129]

---

[129] De Wit, Constant. *Les Inscriptions du Temple d'Opet a Karnak III: Traduction integrale des textes rituels-Essai d'interpretation.* (Bruxelles : Edition de la Fondation Egyptologique Reine Elisabeth, 1968), 88.

INSCRIPTIONS OF SESHAT AND DJEHUTY

Djehuty, the Lord of the Words of God
and Seshat, Who Makes the Writing of the Books.[130]

Djehuty, Lord of Hermopolis and
Seshat, Mistress of Writing.[131]

[130] Budde, Dagmar. *Die Göttin Seschat*. (H. Wodtke & K. Stegbauer, 2000), 73.
[131] Budde, Dagmar. *Die Göttin Seschat*. (H. Wodtke & K. Stegbauer, 2000), 73.

HYMNS TO SESHAT

In Her Name of Sefkhet Abwy

HYMN OF SEFKHET ABWY SESHAT

Sefkhet Abwy Seshat
Lady of Writing
Mistress of the Library
Overseer of the House.[132]

---

[132] Translated from Hafez, Noha Mohamed. "The Scenes of Sefkhet-Abwy at The Temples". *Journal of Association of Arab Universities for Tourism and Hospitality*, 21, 1, 2021, 9.

HYMN OF SEFKHET ABWY

Sefkhet Abwy
Lady of Writing
Lady of the Great God
She Gives All Life, All Power.[133]

---

[133] Translated from Hafez, Noha Mohamed. "The Scenes of Sefkhet-Abwy at The Temples". *Journal of Association of Arab Universities for Tourism and Hospitality*, 21, 1, 2021, 2.

HYMN OF SEFKHET ABWY

Sefkhet Abwy
Lady of Writing
She Who Gives the Writings of Millions of Years
She Who is Foremost in the Library
Given for You all the years of Atum.[134]

---

[134] Translated from Hafez, Noha Mohamed. "The Scenes of Sefkhet-Abwy at The Temples". *Journal of Association of Arab Universities for Tourism and Hospitality*, 21, 1, 2021, 3.

HYMN OF SEFKHET ABWY

Sefkhet Abwy
Lady of Writing
Foremost in the Library.[135]

---

[135] Translated from Hafez, Noha Mohamed. "The Scenes of Sefkhet-Abwy at The Temples". *Journal of Association of Arab Universities for Tourism and Hospitality*, 21, 1, 2021, 3.

Hymn of Sefkhet Abwy

Sefkhet Abwy
Lady of Heaven
Given All Lands,
All Nine Bows united under Your sandals for eternity.[136]

---

[136] Translated from Hafez, Noha Mohamed. "The Scenes of Sefkhet-Abwy at The Temples". *Journal of Association of Arab Universities for Tourism and Hospitality*, 21, 1, 2021, 4.

HYMN OF SEFKHET ABWY

Sefkhet Abwy
Lady of Writing
Mistress of the Library.[137]

---

[137] Translated from Hafez, Noha Mohamed. "The Scenes of Sefkhet-Abwy at The Temples". *Journal of Association of Arab Universities for Tourism and Hospitality*, 21, 1, 2021, 5.

HYMN OF SEFKHET ABWY

Sefkhet Abwy
Lady of Writing
She Gives Life, Stability, Power, and Many Great Jubilees.[138]

---

[138] Translated from Hafez, Noha Mohamed. "The Scenes of Sefkhet-Abwy at The Temples". *Journal of Association of Arab Universities for Tourism and Hospitality*, 21, 1, 2021, 5.

HYMN OF SEFKHET ABWY

Sefkhet Abwy
Lady of Writing
Mistress of the Library
as She gives all life to the King of Upper and Lower Egypt.[139]

---

[139] Translated from Hafez, Noha Mohamed. "The Scenes of Sefkhet-Abwy at The Temples". *Journal of Association of Arab Universities for Tourism and Hospitality*, 21, 1, 2021, 6.

HYMN OF SEFKHET ABWY

Sefkhet Abwy
Lady of Writing
Mistress of the Library
Overseer
Written for you many jubilees.[140]

---

[140] Translated from Hafez, Noha Mohamed. "The Scenes of Sefkhet-Abwy at The Temples". *Journal of Association of Arab Universities for Tourism and Hospitality*, 21, 1, 2021, 9.

HYMN OF SEFKHET ABWY

Sefkhet Abwy
Lady of Writing
Princess of the House of Books
Daughter of Wesir
Who Has Lost Her Reunited Father.[141]

---

[141] Budde, Dagmar. *Die Göttin Seschat*. (H. Wodtke & K. Stegbauer, 2000), 177-178.

HYMNS OF SESHAT SYNCRETISMS

HYMN OF SESHAT OR SESHAT-ASET

Primordial
Who Began Engraving
Seshat, the Great
With Excellent Magic
Princess
Daughter of Geb
Vizir
Daughter of Djehuty
Who Fills the Palace with Perfection
Who Does What is Right Around the Great Seat (Dendera)
Mother of God.[142]

---

[142] Budde, Dagmar. *Die Göttin Seschat*. (H. Wodtke & K. Stegbauer, 2000), 146.

HYMN OF SESHAT-ASET OR ASET-SESHAT

Aset, the Great
Mother of God
Lady of the Temple of Aset
Lady of the Gods
First of Dendera
Seshat, the Great
Princess of Writing
Great of Magic
Lady of the House of Books
Great in the Sky, Powerful on Earth
For Whom the Gods Rise to Worship
Daily.[143]

---

[143] Budde, Dagmar. *Die Göttin Seschat*. (H. Wodtke & K. Stegbauer, 2000), 165.

HYMN OF SESHAT-ASET

Aset, Giver of Life
Mistress of the Abaton
Princess, Mistress of Philae
Seshat, the Great
Princess of the Library
Great of Magic
Princess of All the Gods.[144]

---

[144] Kockelmann, Holger and Erich Winter, *Philae III: Die Zweite Ostkolonnade des Tempels der Isis in Philae. (CO II und CO II K)*, (Verlag der Osterreichischen Akademie der Wissenschaften/Austrian Academy of Sciences, 2016), 143. Translated by Chelsea Bolton. I changed Isis to her ancient Egyptian name Aset.

HYMN OF SESHAT-NEBET HET

Nebet Het
With the Excellent Heart
Small Seshat
Princess of the House of Life.[145]

---

[145] Budde, Dagmar. *Die Göttin Seschat*. (H. Wodtke & K. Stegbauer, 2000), 216.

EXCERPT HYMN OF SESHAT FROM THE NEBET HET HYMN FROM KOMIR TEMPLE

To You, Seshat the Great, Mistress of Men
Mistress of Writing, Lady of the Entire Library
To You,
Who commands the divine decrees
Great of Magic
Who resides in the House of the Archivists.[146]

---

[146] El-Saghir, Mohamed and Dominique Valbelle. "Komir. I. - The Discovery of Komir Temple. Preliminary Report. II. - Deux hymnes aux divinites de Komir : Anoukis et Nephthys." *BIFAO 83* (1983), p. 164-166.

HYMN OF SESHAT-ANUKET

Anuket (Anukis)
Lady of Elephantine
First of Philae
Who Stays in Bigge
Seshat, the Great
Lady of Writing in the House of Books
Great of Magic
Eye of Ra
Lady of the Sky
and Princess of All the Gods.[147]

---

[147] Budde, Dagmar. *Die Göttin Seschat*. (H. Wodtke & K. Stegbauer, 2000), 152.

Excerpt Hymn of Seshat-Hethert

Seshat, the Great
Who Protects Her Brother Wesir
One with the Shining Face
Mistress of Turquoise.[148]

---

[148] Kurth, Dieter. *Edfou VII. Vol. 1-2.* (Otto Harrassowitz Verlag, 2004), 499.

APPENDIXES

Names and Epithets of Seshat

Possible Name Meanings of the Name Seshat

- Female Scribe
- One Who Fixes Fate
- Panther Goddess
- She Who Cares for the Corpse
- She Who Determines the Lifetime
- She Who is the Scribe
- Writer[149]

Ancient Egyptian Praise Name

- Sefkhet—shortened writing of Sefkhet Abwy[150]
- Sefkhet Abwy—Seven Horned; Sevenfold of the Two Horns; She of Seven Points; She Who Has Laid Aside the Two Horns[151]
- Sekhef Abwy—She Who Releases the Two Horns[152]

---

[149] Altenmüller, Hartwig. "Seschat,'die den Leichnam versorgt', als Herrin über Vergangenheit und Geschichte." In Z. Hawass, P. Der Manuelian, R. B. Hussein (Hg.), *Perspectives on Ancient Egypt. Studies in Honor of Edward Brovarski*, Supplément aux Annales du Service des Antiquités de l'Egypte 40, Kairo 2010, S.: 35-37. Hafez, Noha Mohamed. "The Scenes of Sefkhet-Abwy at The Temples". *Journal of Association of Arab Universities for Tourism and Hospitality*, 21, 1, 2021, 1.

[150] Translated from Hafez, Noha Mohamed. "The Scenes of Sefkhet-Abwy at The Temples". *Journal of Association of Arab Universities for Tourism and Hospitality*, 21, 1, 2021, 7.

[151] Hafez, Noha Mohamed. "The Scenes of Sefkhet-Abwy at The Temples". *Journal of Association of Arab Universities for Tourism and Hospitality*, 21, 1, 2021, 1. Butler, Edward. Goddesses and Gods of the Ancient Egyptians: A Theological Encyclopedia: Kindle Edition. (Phaidra Editions, 2021), 277.

Wainwright, G. A. "Seshat and the Pharaoh." in *The Journal of Egyptian Archaeology*, v.26 (February 1941): 31.

[152] Butler, Edward. Goddesses and Gods of the Ancient Egyptians: A Theological Encyclopedia: Kindle Edition. (Phaidra Editions, 2021), 277.

- Shei or Sheit or Shait—the Primeval One[153]

Ancient Egyptian Titles

- Kherseket (in older texts written Kheresket)—She Who Wipes Away Tears[154]
- Merkhetes—She Whose Flame is Painful[155]
- Sopdet (Sothis, Sirius)—the Star Sirius[156]

Forms

- Seshat, the Great
- Seshat, the Small[157]

English Epithets

- At the Side of Him Who Calculates the Dues (Khonsu-Djehuty)[158]
- *Atenet* Who Shines in the Sky[159]
- August *Kherseket* is Seen as the (August) Leader[160]

---

[153] Butler, Edward. <u>Goddesses and Gods of the Ancient Egyptians: A Theological Encyclopedia: Kindle Edition</u>. (Phaidra Editions, 2021), 278.

[154] El-Tonssy, Mohamed A. "The Goddess Rattawy in Greco-Roman Temples." In *The Fifteen Conference Book of the General of Arab Archaeologists*, (2012-2013), pp. 199.

[155] Butler, Edward P. "Opening the Way of Writing: Semiotic Metaphysics in the Book of Thoth." In *Practicing Gnosis*, (Brill, 2013), pp. 229.

[156] Belmonte, Juan Antonio, Miguel Ángel Molinero Polo, and Noemi Miranda. "Unveiling Seshat: New insights into the stretching of the cord ceremony." *In Search of Cosmic Order: Selected Essays on Egyptian Archaeoastronomy* (2009): 204. Budde, Dagmar. <u>Die Göttin Seschat</u>. (H. Wodtke & K. Stegbauer, 2000), 166.

[157] Cauville, Sylvie. <u>Dendara. Le temple d'Isis. Vol. II: Analyse a la lumiere du temple d'Hathor</u>. (Peeters, 2009), 166.

[158] Budde, Dagmar. <u>Die Göttin Seschat</u>. (H. Wodtke & K. Stegbauer, 2000), 159.

[159] Richter, Barbara A., <u>The Theology of Hathor of Dendera: Aural and Visual Scribal Techniques in the Per-Wer Sanctuary,</u> (Lockwood Press, 2016), 341.

[160] El-Tonssy, Mohamed A. "The Goddess Rattawy in Greco-Roman Temples." In *The Fifteen Conference Book of the General of Arab Archaeologists*, (2012-2013), pp. 199. I changed the spelling of "Kheresket" to "Kherseket".

- Before the House of Books of the Royal Offspring[161]
- Controller of the Foreigners of Upper and Lower Egypt[162]
- Before Whom There is Nothing Left[163]
- Daughter of Djehuty[164]
- Daughter of Geb[165]
- Daughter of Wesir[166]
- Excellent Mistress[167]
- Excellent Sister as the Great of Magic[168]
- Excellent Sister of the Great of Magic (Djehuty)[169]
- Eye of Ra[170]
- Female Creator[171]
- Female Djehuty[172]
- Female King of Upper and Lower Egypt[173]
- Female Ruler[174]
- Female Ruler of Papyrus Books[175]
- Female Ruler of Scrolls[176]

---

[161] Wainwright, G. A. "Seshat and the Pharaoh." in *The Journal of Egyptian Archaeology*, v.26 (February 1941): 31.

[162] Wainwright, G. A. "Seshat and the Pharaoh." in *The Journal of Egyptian Archaeology*, v.26 (February 1941): 37.

[163] Budde, Dagmar. *Die Göttin Seschat*. (H. Wodtke & K. Stegbauer, 2000), 166.

[164] Budde, Dagmar. *Die Göttin Seschat*. (H. Wodtke & K. Stegbauer, 2000), 146.

[165] Budde, Dagmar. *Die Göttin Seschat*. (H. Wodtke & K. Stegbauer, 2000), 146.

[166] Budde, Dagmar. *Die Göttin Seschat*. (H. Wodtke & K. Stegbauer, 2000), 177.

[167] Budde, Dagmar. *Die Göttin Seschat*. (H. Wodtke & K. Stegbauer, 2000), 166.

[168] Budde, Dagmar. *Die Göttin Seschat*. (H. Wodtke & K. Stegbauer, 2000), 145. Footnote 17.

[169] Budde, Dagmar. *Die Göttin Seschat*. (H. Wodtke & K. Stegbauer, 2000), 145. Footnote 17.

[170] De Wit, Constant. *Les Inscriptions du Temple d'Opet a Karnak III: Traduction integrale des textes rituels-Essai d'interpretation*. (Bruxelles : Edition de la Fondation Egyptologique Reine Elisabeth, 1968), 88.

[171] Richter, Barbara A., The Theology of Hathor of Dendera: Aural and Visual Scribal Techniques in the Per-Wer Sanctuary, (Lockwood Press, 2016), 261.

[172] Budde, Dagmar. *Die Göttin Seschat*. (H. Wodtke & K. Stegbauer, 2000), 149.

[173] Richter, Barbara A., The Theology of Hathor of Dendera: Aural and Visual Scribal Techniques in the Per-Wer Sanctuary, (Lockwood Press, 2016), 341.

[174] Richter, Barbara A., The Theology of Hathor of Dendera: Aural and Visual Scribal Techniques in the Per-Wer Sanctuary, (Lockwood Press, 2016), 301.

[175] Richter, Barbara A., The Theology of Hathor of Dendera: Aural and Visual Scribal Techniques in the Per-Wer Sanctuary, (Lockwood Press, 2016), 341.

- First of the Archives[177]
- First of the Archive of the Chenmesu Friends[178]
- First of the Archive of the Known Kings[179]
- First of Builders[180]
- First of Dendera[181]
- First of Heseret (Necropolis of Hermopolis Magna)[182]
- First of the House of the Bird Trap[183]
- First of the House of the Book of God[184]
- First of the House of Books[185]
- First of the House of Books and the Royal Workers[186]
- First of the House of the Book of God[187]
- First of the House of Foreigners[188]
- First of the House of Life[189]
- First of the House of Ritual Rules[190]

---

[176] Richter, Barbara A., The Theology of Hathor of Dendera: Aural and Visual Scribal Techniques in the Per-Wer Sanctuary, (Lockwood Press, 2016), 380.

[177] Altenmüller, Hartwig. "Seschat,'die den Leichnam versorgt', als Herrin über Vergangenheit und Geschichte." In Z. Hawass, P. Der Manuelian, R. B. Hussein (Hg.), Perspectives on Ancient Egypt. Studies in Honor of Edward Brovarski, Supplément aux Annales du Service des Antiquités de l'Egypte 40, Kairo 2010, S.: 45.

[178] Altenmüller, Hartwig. "Seschat,'die den Leichnam versorgt', als Herrin über Vergangenheit und Geschichte." In Z. Hawass, P. Der Manuelian, R. B. Hussein (Hg.), Perspectives on Ancient Egypt. Studies in Honor of Edward Brovarski, Supplément aux Annales du Service des Antiquités de l'Egypte 40, Kairo 2010, S.: 45.

[179] Altenmüller, Hartwig. "Seschat,'die den Leichnam versorgt', als Herrin über Vergangenheit und Geschichte." In Z. Hawass, P. Der Manuelian, R. B. Hussein (Hg.), Perspectives on Ancient Egypt. Studies in Honor of Edward Brovarski, Supplément aux Annales du Service des Antiquités de l'Egypte 40, Kairo 2010, S.: 45.

[180] Budde, Dagmar. Die Göttin Seschat. (H. Wodtke & K. Stegbauer, 2000), 25.

[181] Budde, Dagmar. Die Göttin Seschat. (H. Wodtke & K. Stegbauer, 2000), 166.

[182] Budde, Dagmar. Die Göttin Seschat. (H. Wodtke & K. Stegbauer, 2000), 27.

[183] Budde, Dagmar. Die Göttin Seschat. (H. Wodtke & K. Stegbauer, 2000), 145.

[184] Budde, Dagmar. Die Göttin Seschat. (H. Wodtke & K. Stegbauer, 2000), 203.

[185] Budde, Dagmar. Die Göttin Seschat. (H. Wodtke & K. Stegbauer, 2000), 20.

[186] Budde, Dagmar. Die Göttin Seschat. (H. Wodtke & K. Stegbauer, 2000), 67.

[187] Altenmüller, Hartwig. "Seschat,'die den Leichnam versorgt', als Herrin über Vergangenheit und Geschichte." In Z. Hawass, P. Der Manuelian, R. B. Hussein (Hg.), Perspectives on Ancient Egypt. Studies in Honor of Edward Brovarski, Supplément aux Annales du Service des Antiquités de l'Egypte 40, Kairo 2010, S.: 45.

[188] Budde, Dagmar. Die Göttin Seschat. (H. Wodtke & K. Stegbauer, 2000), 206. Footnote 49.

[189] Budde, Dagmar. Die Göttin Seschat. (H. Wodtke & K. Stegbauer, 2000), 205.

- First of the Library[191]
- First of Philae[192]
- First Who Wrote[193]
- Flower of Ra in His Hand[194]
- For Whom the Gods Rise to Worship Daily[195]
- Foremost of the House of Books[196]
- Foremost of the House of Life[197]
- Foremost of the Library[198]
- Foremost of the Temple[199]
- Foremost One of the Chamber of Darkness[200]
- Gold[201]
- Great[202]
- Great, Mistress of the House of Books[203]
- Great, Mistress of Writing, First of the House of Books[204]
- Great Mother of the Writings[205]

---

[190] Budde, Dagmar. *Die Göttin Seschat*. (H. Wodtke & K. Stegbauer, 2000), 24.

[191] Budde, Dagmar. *Die Göttin Seschat*. (H. Wodtke & K. Stegbauer, 2000), 25.

[192] Budde, Dagmar. *Die Göttin Seschat*. (H. Wodtke & K. Stegbauer, 2000), 152.

[193] Cauville, Sylvie, Le Temple de Dendera: La Porte d'Isis, Dendara. (Cairo: IFAO, 1999), 99.

[194] Budde, Dagmar. *Die Göttin Seschat*. (H. Wodtke & K. Stegbauer, 2000), 182.

[195] Budde, Dagmar. *Die Göttin Seschat*. (H. Wodtke & K. Stegbauer, 2000), 165.

[196] Magdolen, Dusan. "A New Investigation of the Symbol of Ancient Egyptian Goddess Seschat." in *Asian and African Studies, v.18 no.2* (12/2009): 173.

[197] Magdolen, Dusan. "A New Investigation of the Symbol of Ancient Egyptian Goddess Seschat." in *Asian and African Studies, v.18 no.2* (12/2009): 173.

[198] Translated from Hafez, Noha Mohamed. "The Scenes of Sefkhet-Abwy at The Temples". *Journal of Association of Arab Universities for Tourism and Hospitality*, 21, 1, 2021, 7-8.

[199] Translated from Hafez, Noha Mohamed. "The Scenes of Sefkhet-Abwy at The Temples". *Journal of Association of Arab Universities for Tourism and Hospitality*, 21, 1, 2021, 7.

[200] Butler, Edward. Goddesses and Gods of the Ancient Egyptians: A Theological Encyclopedia: Kindle Edition. (Phaidra Editions, 2021), 278. From the Temple of Edfu.

[201] Westendorf, Wolfhart. "Beiträge aus und zu den medizinischen Texten." *Zeitschrift für ägyptische Sprache und Altertumskunde* 92, no. 1 (1966): 137-139. Budde, Dagmar. *Die Göttin Seschat*. (H. Wodtke & K. Stegbauer, 2000), 5.

[202] Kockelmann, Holger and Erich Winter. Philae III: Die Zweite Ostkolonnade des Tempels der Isis in Philae. (CO II und CO II K). (Verlag der Osterreichischen Akademie der Wissenschaften/Austrian Academy of Sciences, 2016), 91.

[203] Budde, Dagmar. *Die Göttin Seschat*. (H. Wodtke & K. Stegbauer, 2000), 157.

[204] Budde, Dagmar. *Die Göttin Seschat*. (H. Wodtke & K. Stegbauer, 2000), 98.

- Great Lady of Writing[206]
- Great of Magic[207]
- Great of Magic in the House of Books[208]
- Great of Magic, Princess of the House of Books[209]
- Guarded in Her Vicinity[210]
- Head of the Library[211]
- Headmistress of the House of Books[212]
- Headmistress of the House of the Books of God[213]
- Headmistress of the House of Ritual Rules[214]
- Huntress[215]
- In Hermpolis Magna[216]
- In Hermopolis Parva[217]
- In the House of Books[218]
- In the House of Seshat[219]

---

[205] Butler, Edward P. "Opening the Way of Writing: Semiotic Metaphysics in the Book of Thoth." In *Practicing Gnosis*, (Brill, 2013), pp. 230. Jasnow, Richard, and Karl-Theodor Zauzich. The Ancient Egyptian Book of Thoth: A Demotic Discourse on Knowledge and Pendant to the Classical Hermetica. (Wiesbaden: Harrassowitz Verlag, 2005), 332. From the *Book of Thoth*, BO2, 3/9.

[206] El-Tonssy, Mohamed A. "The Goddess Rattawy in Greco-Roman Temples." In *The Fifteen Conference Book of the General of Arab Archaeologists*, (2012-2013), pp. 199.

[207] Kockelmann, Holger and Erich Winter. Philae III: Die Zweite Ostkolonnade des Tempels der Isis in Philae. (CO II und CO II K). (Verlag der Osterreichischen Akademie der Wissenschaften/Austrian Academy of Sciences, 2016), 143.

[208] Budde, Dagmar. *Die Göttin Seschat*. (H. Wodtke & K. Stegbauer, 2000), 101.

[209] Budde, Dagmar. *Die Göttin Seschat*. (H. Wodtke & K. Stegbauer, 2000), 100.

[210] Kockelmann, Holger and Erich Winter, *Philae III: Die Zweite Ostkolonnade des Tempels der Isis in Philae. (CO II und CO II K)*, (Verlag der Osterreichischen Akademie der Wissenschaften/Austrian Academy of Sciences, 2016), 141.

[211] Hafez, Noha Mohamed. "The Scenes of Sefkhet-Abwy at The Temples". *Journal of Association of Arab Universities for Tourism and Hospitality*, 21, 1, 2021, 6. I added "the" to the "Chief of Library" for clarity.

[212] Budde, Dagmar. *Die Göttin Seschat*. (H. Wodtke & K. Stegbauer, 2000), 194.

[213] Budde, Dagmar. *Die Göttin Seschat*. (H. Wodtke & K. Stegbauer, 2000), 204.

[214] Budde, Dagmar. *Die Göttin Seschat*. (H. Wodtke & K. Stegbauer, 2000), 194.

[215] Butler, Edward. Goddesses and Gods of the Ancient Egyptians: A Theological Encyclopedia: Kindle Edition. (Phaidra Editions, 2021), 278.

[216] Budde, Dagmar. *Die Göttin Seschat*. (H. Wodtke & K. Stegbauer, 2000), 61.

[217] Budde, Dagmar. *Die Göttin Seschat*. (H. Wodtke & K. Stegbauer, 2000), 61.

[218] Budde, Dagmar. *Die Göttin Seschat*. (H. Wodtke & K. Stegbauer, 2000), 207.

- Keeper of Memories[220]
- King's Mother[221]
- Lady of Books[222]
- Lady of Builders[223]
- Lady of Djehuty (Thoth), the Overseer[224]
- Lady of Elephantine[225]
- Lady of the Gods[226]
- Lady of Heaven[227]
- Lady of Hermopolis[228]
- Lady of Hieroglyphs[229]
- Lady of the House of Books[230]
- Lady of the Library[231]
- Lady of the Palace[232]
- Lady of Scripture[233]
- Lady of the Sky[234]
- Lady of the Stars[235]

---

[219] Budde, Dagmar. *Die Göttin Seschat*. (H. Wodtke & K. Stegbauer, 2000), 58.

[220] Hafez, Noha Mohamed. "The Scenes of Sefkhet-Abwy at The Temples". *Journal of Association of Arab Universities for Tourism and Hospitality*, 21, 1, 2021, 1.

[221] Budde, Dagmar. *Die Göttin Seschat*. (H. Wodtke & K. Stegbauer, 2000), 163.

[222] Siuda, Tamara L. *Nebt Het: Lady of the House*. (Stargazer Design, 2010), 11.

[223] Magdolen, Dusan. "A New Investigation of the Symbol of Ancient Egyptian Goddess Seshat." in *Asian and African Studies*, v.18 no.2 (12/2009): 173.

[224] Hafez, Noha Mohamed. "The Scenes of Sefkhet-Abwy at The Temples". *Journal of Association of Arab Universities for Tourism and Hospitality*, 21, 1, 2021, 7.

[225] Budde, Dagmar. *Die Göttin Seschat*. (H. Wodtke & K. Stegbauer, 2000), 152.

[226] Budde, Dagmar. *Die Göttin Seschat*. (H. Wodtke & K. Stegbauer, 2000), 99.

[227] Hafez, Noha Mohamed. "The Scenes of Sefkhet-Abwy at The Temples". *Journal of Association of Arab Universities for Tourism and Hospitality*, 21, 1, 2021, 11.

[228] Budde, Dagmar. *Die Göttin Seschat*. (H. Wodtke & K. Stegbauer, 2000), 144.

[229] Magdolen, Dusan. "A New Investigation of the Symbol of Ancient Egyptian Goddess Seshat." in *Asian and African Studies*, v.18 no.2 (12/2009): 173.

[230] Budde, Dagmar. *Die Göttin Seschat*. (H. Wodtke & K. Stegbauer, 2000), 165.

[231] Hafez, Noha Mohamed. "The Scenes of Sefkhet-Abwy at The Temples". *Journal of Association of Arab Universities for Tourism and Hospitality*, 21, 1, 2021, 7 and 11.

[232] Budde, Dagmar. *Die Göttin Seschat*. (H. Wodtke & K. Stegbauer, 2000), 84. Footnote 127.

[233] Kockelmann, Holger and Erich Winter. *Philae III: Die Zweite Ostkolonnade des Tempels der Isis in Philae. (CO II und CO II K)*. (Verlag der Osterreichischen Akademie der Wissenschaften/Austrian Academy of Sciences, 2016), 91.

[234] Budde, Dagmar. *Die Göttin Seschat*. (H. Wodtke & K. Stegbauer, 2000), 99.

- Lady of the Temple of Aset[236]
- Lady of the Transfigurations of Ra[237]
- Lady of the Walls[238]
- Lady of the Words of God[239]
- Lady of Writing[240]
- Lady of Writings in the House of Life[241]
- Lady of Years[242]
- Magnificent in the House of Life[243]
- Magnificent, Ruler, Princess of the Goddesses[244]
- Mistress of Archives[245]
- Mistress of Builders[246]
- Mistress of the Drummers[247]
- Mistress of Elephantine[248]
- Mistress of the Headmistress[249]

---

[235] Budde, Dagmar. *Die Göttin Seschat*. (H. Wodtke & K. Stegbauer, 2000), 229.

[236] Budde, Dagmar. *Die Göttin Seschat*. (H. Wodtke & K. Stegbauer, 2000), 166.

[237] Budde, Dagmar. *Die Göttin Seschat*. (H. Wodtke & K. Stegbauer, 2000), 148.

[238] Siuda, Tamara L. Ancient Egyptian Daybook. (Stargazer Design, 2016), 99.

[239] Budde, Dagmar. *Die Göttin Seschat*. (H. Wodtke & K. Stegbauer, 2000), 27.

[240] Magdolen, Dusan. "A New Investigation of the Symbol of Ancient Egyptian Goddess Seshat." in *Asian and African Studies*, v.18 no.2 (12/2009): 173. Cauville, Sylvie, Le Temple de Dendera: La Porte d'Isis, Dendara. (Cairo: IFAO, 1999), 99.

[241] Wainwright, G. A. "Seshat and the Pharaoh." in *The Journal of Egyptian Archaeology*, v.26 (February 1941): 31.

[242] Budde, Dagmar. *Die Göttin Seschat*. (H. Wodtke & K. Stegbauer, 2000), 21.

[243] Budde, Dagmar. *Die Göttin Seschat*. (H. Wodtke & K. Stegbauer, 2000), 59.

[244] Budde, Dagmar. *Die Göttin Seschat*. (H. Wodtke & K. Stegbauer, 2000), 157.

[245] Altenmüller, Hartwig. "Seschat,'die den Leichnam versorgt', als Herrin über Vergangenheit und Geschichte." In Z. Hawass, P. Der Manuelian, R. B. Hussein (Hg.), *Perspectives on Ancient Egypt. Studies in Honor of Edward Brovarski*, Supplément aux Annales du Service des Antiquités de l'Egypte 40, Kairo 2010, S.: 45.

[246] Altenmüller, Hartwig. "Seschat,'die den Leichnam versorgt', als Herrin über Vergangenheit und Geschichte." In Z. Hawass, P. Der Manuelian, R. B. Hussein (Hg.), *Perspectives on Ancient Egypt. Studies in Honor of Edward Brovarski*, Supplément aux Annales du Service des Antiquités de l'Egypte 40, Kairo 2010, S.: 46.

[247] Altenmüller, Hartwig. "Seschat,'die den Leichnam versorgt', als Herrin über Vergangenheit und Geschichte." In Z. Hawass, P. Der Manuelian, R. B. Hussein (Hg.), *Perspectives on Ancient Egypt. Studies in Honor of Edward Brovarski*, Supplément aux Annales du Service des Antiquités de l'Egypte 40, Kairo 2010, S.: 45.

[248] Budde, Dagmar. *Die Göttin Seschat*. (H. Wodtke & K. Stegbauer, 2000), 27.

- Mistress of Goddesses[250]
- Mistress of His Lip[251]
- Mistress of Heseret (Necropolis of Hermopolis Magna)[252]
- Mistress of the House of Books[253]
- Mistress of the House of Ritual Rules[254]
- Mistress of the House of *Rwtjw*[255]
- Mistress of the House of Writing[256]
- Mistress of the Library[257]
- Mistress of the Plans in the Temples[258]
- Mistress of Potters[259]
- Mistress of the Rope[260]
- Mistress of the Rope, Foremost One of the Chamber of Darkness[261]

---

[249] Budde, Dagmar. *Die Göttin Seschat*. (H. Wodtke & K. Stegbauer, 2000), 193.

1. [250] Richter, Barbara A., The Theology of Hathor of Dendera: Aural and Visual Scribal Techniques in the Per-Wer Sanctuary, (Lockwood Press, 2016), 301.

2.
[251] Budde, Dagmar. *Die Göttin Seschat*. (H. Wodtke & K. Stegbauer, 2000), 224.

[252] Budde, Dagmar. *Die Göttin Seschat*. (H. Wodtke & K. Stegbauer, 2000), 27.

[253] Wainwright, G. A. "Seshat and the Pharaoh." in *The Journal of Egyptian Archaeology*, v.26 (February 1941): 31.

[254] Altenmüller, Hartwig. "Seschat,'die den Leichnam versorgt', als Herrin über Vergangenheit und Geschichte." In Z. Hawass, P. Der Manuelian, R. B. Hussein (Hg.), *Perspectives on Ancient Egypt. Studies in Honor of Edward Brovarski*, Supplément aux Annales du Service des Antiquités de l'Egypte 40, Kairo 2010, S.: 45.

[255] Altenmüller, Hartwig. "Seschat,'die den Leichnam versorgt', als Herrin über Vergangenheit und Geschichte." In Z. Hawass, P. Der Manuelian, R. B. Hussein (Hg.), *Perspectives on Ancient Egypt. Studies in Honor of Edward Brovarski*, Supplément aux Annales du Service des Antiquités de l'Egypte 40, Kairo 2010, S.: 45.

[256] Cauville, Sylvie. Dendara. Le temple d'Isis. Vol. II: Analyse a la lumiere du temple d'Hathor. (Peeters, 2009), 262.

[257] El-Tonssy, Mohamed A. "The Goddess Rattawy in Greco-Roman Temples." In *The Fifteen Conference Book of the General of Arab Archaeologists*, (2012-2013), pp. 197. I spelled Rattawy as Raettawy. I left out "is the" in the first line. I changed "Mistress of Library" to "Mistress of the Library".

[258] Budde, Dagmar. *Die Göttin Seschat*. (H. Wodtke & K. Stegbauer, 2000), 194.

[259] Siuda, Tamara L. in The Ancient Egyptian Prayerbook. (Stargazer Design, 2009), 73.

[260] Butler, Edward. Goddesses and Gods of the Ancient Egyptians: A Theological Encyclopedia: Kindle Edition. (Phaidra Editions, 2021), 278. From Temple of Edfu.

[261] Butler, Edward. Goddesses and Gods of the Ancient Egyptians: A Theological Encyclopedia: Kindle Edition. (Phaidra Editions, 2021), 278. From Temple of Edfu.

- Mistress of Scripture[262]
- Mistress of the Scratching of the Ground Plan in the Great Seat (Edfu)[263]
- Mistress of the Sky[264]
- Mistress of the Temple[265]
- Mistress of the Tongue Which Acts Against Poison[266]
- Mistress of Turquoise[267]
- Mistress of Walking in the Palace[268]
- Mistress of the Wall(s)[269]
- Mistress of What is Written in the House of Ritual Rules[270]
- Mistress of Writing[271]
- Mistress of Writing and the Mistress of the Words of God[272]
- Mistress of Writing in the House of Books[273]
- Mistress of Writing, Lady of the Sky and Princess of the Gods[274]
- Mistress of Writing, the Soul Incarnated in the Scriptorium[275]
- Mistress of Years[276]
- Mother[277]

---

[262] Altenmüller, Hartwig. "Seschat,'die den Leichnam versorgt', als Herrin über Vergangenheit und Geschichte." In Z. Hawass, P. Der Manuelian, R. B. Hussein (Hg.), *Perspectives on Ancient Egypt. Studies in Honor of Edward Brovarski*, Supplément aux Annales du Service des Antiquités de l'Egypte 40, Kairo 2010, S.: 46.

[263] Budde, Dagmar. *Die Göttin Seschat*. (H. Wodtke & K. Stegbauer, 2000), 195.

[264] De Wit, Constant. *Les Inscriptions du Temple d'Opet a Karnak III: Traduction integrale des textes rituels–Essai d'interpretation.* (Bruxelles : Edition de la Fondation Egyptologique Reine Elisabeth, 1968), 88.

[265] Budde, Dagmar. *Die Göttin Seschat*. (H. Wodtke & K. Stegbauer, 2000), 199.

[266] Budde, Dagmar. *Die Göttin Seschat*. (H. Wodtke & K. Stegbauer, 2000), 224.

[267] Kurth, Dieter. *Edfou VII. Vol. 1-2.* (Otto Harrassowitz Verlag, 2004), 499.

[268] Budde, Dagmar. *Die Göttin Seschat*. (H. Wodtke & K. Stegbauer, 2000), 120.

[269] Siuda, Tamara L. Ancient Egyptian Daybook. (Stargazer Design, 2016), 238.

[270] Budde, Dagmar. *Die Göttin Seschat*. (H. Wodtke & K. Stegbauer, 2000), 120.

[271] Hafez, Noha Mohamed. "The Scenes of Sefkhet-Abwy at The Temples". *Journal of Association of Arab Universities for Tourism and Hospitality*, 21, 1, 2021, 11.

[272] Budde, Dagmar. *Die Göttin Seschat*. (H. Wodtke & K. Stegbauer, 2000), 200.

[273] Budde, Dagmar. *Die Göttin Seschat*. (H. Wodtke & K. Stegbauer, 2000), 120.

[274] Budde, Dagmar. *Die Göttin Seschat*. (H. Wodtke & K. Stegbauer, 2000), 99.

[275] Cauville, Sylvie. Dendara. Le temple d'Isis. Vol. II: Analyse a la lumiere du temple d'Hathor. (Peeters, 2009), 261.

[276] Budde, Dagmar. *Die Göttin Seschat*. (H. Wodtke & K. Stegbauer, 2000), 111.

- Mother of God[278]
- Mother of God in the Birth House[279]
- Mother of Writing[280]
- Noble Lady[281]
- Noble and Powerful Lady[282]
- Of Lower Egypt[283]
- One Who First Established the Chamber[284]
- One Who Found the Temples with Their Cult Images[285]
- One Who Provides the Texts[286]
- One with the Shining Face[287]
- Overseer[288]
- Overseer of the House[289]
- Original One[290]
- Original One, Who Originated Writing at the Beginning[291]

---

[277] Butler, Edward. Goddesses and Gods of the Ancient Egyptians: A Theological Encyclopedia: Kindle Edition. (Phaidra Editions, 2021), 278. In Coffin Texts Spell 68.

[278] Budde, Dagmar. Die Göttin Seschat. (H. Wodtke & K. Stegbauer, 2000), 146.

[279] Cauville, Sylvie, Le Temple de Dendera: La Porte d'Isis, Dendara. (Cairo: IFAO, 1999), 99.

[280] Butler, Edward P. "Opening the Way of Writing: Semiotic Metaphysics in the Book of Thoth." In Practicing Gnosis, (Brill, 2013), pp. 230. Jasnow, Richard, and Karl-Theodor Zauzich. The Ancient Egyptian Book of Thoth: A Demotic Discourse on Knowledge and Pendant to the Classical Hermetica. (Wiesbaden: Harrassowitz Verlag, 2005), 332. From the Book of Thoth, BO2, 3/9.

[281] Richter, Barbara A., The Theology of Hathor of Dendera: Aural and Visual Scribal Techniques in the Per-Wer Sanctuary, (Lockwood Press, 2016), 301.

[282] Richter, Barbara A., The Theology of Hathor of Dendera: Aural and Visual Scribal Techniques in the Per-Wer Sanctuary, (Lockwood Press, 2016), 341.

[283] Budde, Dagmar. Die Göttin Seschat. (H. Wodtke & K. Stegbauer, 2000), 59.

[284] Butler, Edward P. "Opening the Way of Writing: Semiotic Metaphysics in the Book of Thoth." In Practicing Gnosis, (Brill, 2013), pp. 251.

[285] Budde, Dagmar. Die Göttin Seschat. (H. Wodtke & K. Stegbauer, 2000), 27.

[286] Kockelmann, Holger and Erich Winter, Philae III: Die Zweite Ostkolonnade des Tempels der Isis in Philae. (CO II und CO II K), (Verlag der Osterreichischen Akademie der Wissenschaften/Austrian Academy of Sciences, 2016), 141.

[287] Kurth, Dieter. Edfou VII. Vol. 1-2. (Otto Harrassowitz Verlag, 2004), 499.

[288] Hafez, Noha Mohamed. "The Scenes of Sefkhet-Abwy at The Temples". Journal of Association of Arab Universities for Tourism and Hospitality, 21, 1, 2021, 7.

[289] Hafez, Noha Mohamed. "The Scenes of Sefkhet-Abwy at The Temples". Journal of Association of Arab Universities for Tourism and Hospitality, 21, 1, 2021, 7 and 11.

[290] Wainwright, G. A. "Seshat and the Pharaoh." in The Journal of Egyptian Archaeology, v.26 (February 1941): 31.

- Perfect Renenutet in the House of Heru (Edfu)[292]
- Preeminent One in the Archive of Those Concerned with the Affairs of the King[293]
- Primeval One[294]
- Primordial[295]
- Primordial One[296]
- Primordial One, Who Invented Writing[297]
- Princess[298]
- Princess of All the Gods[299]
- Princess of the Goddesses[300]
- Princess of the House of Books[301]
- Princess of the House of Life[302]
- Princess in the House of Ritual Rules[303]
- Princess of Knitting[304]
- Princess of the Library[305]

---

[291] Wainwright, G. A. "Seshat and the Pharaoh." in *The Journal of Egyptian Archaeology, v.26* (February 1941): 31.

[292] Budde, Dagmar. *Die Göttin Seshat*. (H. Wodtke & K. Stegbauer, 2000), 120.

[293] Magdolen, Dušan. "The Development of the Sign of the Ancient Egyptian Goddess Seshat Down to the End of the Old Kingdom: Analysis and Interpretation." *Asian and African Studies* 15, no. 1 (2006): 72.

[294] Butler, Edward. Goddesses and Gods of the Ancient Egyptians: A Theological Encyclopedia: Kindle Edition. (Phaidra Editions, 2021), 278.

[295] Budde, Dagmar. *Die Göttin Seshat*. (H. Wodtke & K. Stegbauer, 2000), 146.

3. [296] Cauville, Sylvie, Le Temple de Dendera: La Porte d'Isis, Dendara. (Cairo: IFAO, 1999), 99. Richter, Barbara A., The Theology of Hathor of Dendera: Aural and Visual Scribal Techniques in the Per-Wer Sanctuary, (Lockwood Press, 2016), 503.

[297] Cauville, Sylvie. Dendara. Le temple d'Isis. Vol. II: Analyse a la lumiere du temple d'Hathor. (Peeters, 2009), 262.

[298] Budde, Dagmar. *Die Göttin Seshat*. (H. Wodtke & K. Stegbauer, 2000), 146.

[299] Kockelmann, Holger and Erich Winter. Philae III: Die Zweite Ostkolonnade des Tempels der Isis in Philae. (CO II und CO II K). (Verlag der Osterreichischen Akademie der Wissenschaften/Austrian Academy of Sciences, 2016), 143.

[300] Budde, Dagmar. *Die Göttin Seshat*. (H. Wodtke & K. Stegbauer, 2000), 157.

[301] Budde, Dagmar. *Die Göttin Seshat*. (H. Wodtke & K. Stegbauer, 2000), 193.

[302] Budde, Dagmar. *Die Göttin Seshat*. (H. Wodtke & K. Stegbauer, 2000), 205.

[303] Budde, Dagmar. *Die Göttin Seshat*. (H. Wodtke & K. Stegbauer, 2000), 59.

[304] Budde, Dagmar. *Die Göttin Seshat*. (H. Wodtke & K. Stegbauer, 2000), 195.

[305] Kockelmann, Holger and Erich Winter. Philae III: Die Zweite Ostkolonnade des Tempels der Isis in Philae. (CO II und CO II K). (Verlag der Osterreichischen Akademie der

- Princess and Ruler of the Founding of the Temples[306]
- Princess of the Two Lands[307]
- Princess of Writing[308]
- Protector[309]
- Protector of the Library of Alexandria[310]
- Pure[311]
- Ruler of the Books[312]
- Ruler and Mistress of Writing[313]
- Seven-Horned[314]
- Seven-Horned, Lady of the Walls[315]
- She Being a Lamp of Prophecy[316]
- She of Heru[317]
- She Notches or Carves the Years of the Life-Period[318]
- She Who is Foremost in the Library[319]
- She Who protects the Sun God with Her Chosen Spells[320]
- She Who is Wise[321]

Wissenschaften/Austrian Academy of Sciences, 2016), 91 and 143. Budde, Dagmar. _Die Göttin Seschat_. (H. Wodtke & K. Stegbauer, 2000), 25.

[306] Budde, Dagmar. _Die Göttin Seschat_. (H. Wodtke & K. Stegbauer, 2000), 27.

[307] Budde, Dagmar. _Die Göttin Seschat_. (H. Wodtke & K. Stegbauer, 2000), 26.

[308] Budde, Dagmar. _Die Göttin Seschat_. (H. Wodtke & K. Stegbauer, 2000), 25.

[309] Hafez, Noha Mohamed. "The Scenes of Sefkhet-Abwy at The Temples". _Journal of Association of Arab Universities for Tourism and Hospitality_, 21, 1, 2021, 7.

[310] Hafez, Noha Mohamed. "The Scenes of Sefkhet-Abwy at The Temples". _Journal of Association of Arab Universities for Tourism and Hospitality_, 21, 1, 2021, 1.

[311] Budde, Dagmar. _Die Göttin Seschat_. (H. Wodtke & K. Stegbauer, 2000), 165.

[312] Budde, Dagmar. _Die Göttin Seschat_. (H. Wodtke & K. Stegbauer, 2000), 27.

[313] Budde, Dagmar. _Die Göttin Seschat_. (H. Wodtke & K. Stegbauer, 2000), 20.

[314] Siuda, Tamara L. _Ancient Egyptian Daybook._ (Stargazer Design, 2016), 99.

[315] Siuda, Tamara L. _Ancient Egyptian Daybook._ (Stargazer Design, 2016), 99.

[316] Butler, Edward P. "Opening the Way of Writing: Semiotic Metaphysics in the Book of Thoth." In _Practicing Gnosis_, (Brill, 2013), pp. 251.

[317] Dunand, Francoise. _Le Culte D'Isis Et Les Ptolémées._ (Netherlands: Brill, 2015), 8.

[318] Wainwright, G. A. "Seshat and the Pharaoh." in _The Journal of Egyptian Archaeology_, v.26 (February 1941): 31.

[319] Pinch, Geraldine. _Egyptian Mythology: A Guide to the Gods, Goddesses and Traditions of Ancient Egypt._ (New York: Oxford University Press, 2004), 190.

[320] El-Tonssy, Mohamed A. "The Goddess Rattawy in Greco-Roman Temples." In _The Fifteen Conference Book of the General of Arab Archaeologists_, (2012-2013), pp. 197.

- She Who Wipes Away Tears[322]
- She Whose Flame is Painful[323]
- Sister of Djehuty[324]
- Sopdet, Who Makes Wesir Young[325]
- Sovereign and Mistress of Writing[326]
- Sovereign of the House of Books[327]
- Stretches the Cord of the Palace[328]
- Trapper[329]
- Twin Sisters (with Mafdet)[330]
- Vizir[331]
- Wet Nurse of Heru by Her Spells[332]
- What Goes Forth From Her Mouth Comes into Being at Once[333]
- Who Began Engraving[334]

[321] Butler, Edward P. "Opening the Way of Writing: Semiotic Metaphysics in the Book of Thoth." In *Practicing Gnosis*, (Brill, 2013), pp. 251.
[322] El-Tonssy, Mohamed A. "The Goddess Rattawy in Greco-Roman Temples." In *The Fifteen Conference Book of the General of Arab Archaeologists*, (2012-2013), pp. 199.
[323] Butler, Edward P. "Opening the Way of Writing: Semiotic Metaphysics in the Book of Thoth." In *Practicing Gnosis*, (Brill, 2013), pp. 229.
[324] Budde, Dagmar. <u>Die Göttin Seschat</u>. (H. Wodtke & K. Stegbauer, 2000), 145.
[325] Budde, Dagmar. <u>Die Göttin Seschat</u>. (H. Wodtke & K. Stegbauer, 2000), 166.
[326] Cauville, Sylvie. <u>Dendara. Le temple d'Isis. Vol. II: Analyse a la lumiere du temple d'Hathor</u>. (Peeters, 2009), 262.
[327] De Wit, Constant. *Les Inscriptions du Temple d'Opet a Karnak III: Traduction integrale des textes rituels-Essai d'interpretation.* (Bruxelles : Edition de la Fondation Egyptologique Reine Elisabeth, 1968), 88.
[328] El-Tonssy, Mohamed A. "The Goddess Rattawy in Greco-Roman Temples." In *The Fifteen Conference Book of the General of Arab Archaeologists*, (2012-2013), pp. 199.
[329] Butler, Edward. <u>Goddesses and Gods of the Ancient Egyptians: A Theological Encyclopedia: Kindle Edition</u>. (Phaidra Editions, 2021), 278.
[330] Westendorf,Wolfhart. "Beiträge aus und zu den medizinischen Texten." *Zeitschrift für ägyptische Sprache und Altertumskunde* 92, no. 1 (1966): 136.
[331] Budde, Dagmar. <u>Die Göttin Seschat</u>. (H. Wodtke & K. Stegbauer, 2000), 146.
[332] El-Tonssy, Mohamed A. "The Goddess Rattawy in Greco-Roman Temples." In *The Fifteen Conference Book of the General of Arab Archaeologists*, (2012-2013), pp. 197. I spelled Rattawy as Raettawy. I left out "is the" in the first line. I changed "Mistress of Library" to "Mistress of the Library".
[333] Richter, Barbara A., <u>The Theology of Hathor of Dendera: Aural and Visual Scribal Techniques in the Per-Wer Sanctuary,</u> (Lockwood Press, 2016), 341.
[334] Budde, Dagmar. <u>Die Göttin Seschat</u>. (H. Wodtke & K. Stegbauer, 2000), 146.

- Who Began Engraving Among the Goddesses[335]
- Who Calculates All Things[336]
- Who Calculates His (Djehuty)'s Command[337]
- Who Created Writing[338]
- Who Does What is Right Around the Great Seat (Dendera)[339]
- Who Dwells in the Temple of Sethos, the First[340]
- Who Fills the Palace with Perfection[341]
- Who Founded the Places of Worship Through Her Prescriptions[342]
- Who Gives Orders in the Palace[343]
- Who Gives to Whom She Loves[344]
- Who Grants Her Son Harpokrates Numerous Years[345]
- Who Has Begun to Tighten the Ropes at the Places[346]
- Who is in the Heart of the Temple of Behdet (Edfu)[347]
- Who is Pure in the House of Rituals[348]
- Who is at the Side of Him Who Knows Egypt (Djehuty)[349]
- Who Invented Writing[350]
- Who Initiated Writing[351]

[335] Budde, Dagmar. _Die Göttin Seschat_. (H. Wodtke & K. Stegbauer, 2000), 168.
[336] Budde, Dagmar. _Die Göttin Seschat_. (H. Wodtke & K. Stegbauer, 2000), 122.
[337] Budde, Dagmar. _Die Göttin Seschat_. (H. Wodtke & K. Stegbauer, 2000), 159.
[338] Richter, Barbara A., The Theology of Hathor of Dendera: Aural and Visual Scribal Techniques in the Per-Wer Sanctuary, (Lockwood Press, 2016), 341.
[339] Budde, Dagmar. _Die Göttin Seschat_. (H. Wodtke & K. Stegbauer, 2000), 146.
[340] Budde, Dagmar. _Die Göttin Seschat_. (H. Wodtke & K. Stegbauer, 2000), 145.
[341] Budde, Dagmar. _Die Göttin Seschat_. (H. Wodtke & K. Stegbauer, 2000), 146.
[342] Cauville, Sylvie. Dendara. Le temple d'Isis. Vol. II: Analyse a la lumiere du temple d'Hathor. (Peeters, 2009), 261.
[343] Budde, Dagmar. _Die Göttin Seschat_. (H. Wodtke & K. Stegbauer, 2000), 201.
[344] Budde, Dagmar. _Die Göttin Seschat_. (H. Wodtke & K. Stegbauer, 2000), 111.
[345] Budde, Dagmar. _Die Göttin Seschat_. (H. Wodtke & K. Stegbauer, 2000), 155.
[346] Budde, Dagmar. _Die Göttin Seschat_. (H. Wodtke & K. Stegbauer, 2000), 27.
[347] Translated from Hafez, Noha Mohamed. "The Scenes of Sefkhet-Abwy at The Temples". _Journal of Association of Arab Universities for Tourism and Hospitality_, 21, 1, 2021, 7.
[348] Budde, Dagmar. _Die Göttin Seschat_. (H. Wodtke & K. Stegbauer, 2000), 165.
[349] Budde, Dagmar. _Die Göttin Seschat_. (H. Wodtke & K. Stegbauer, 2000), 166.
[350] Richter, Barbara A., The Theology of Hathor of Dendera: Aural and Visual Scribal Techniques in the Per-Wer Sanctuary, (Lockwood Press, 2016), 380.

- Who Lives in the House of the Dancers[352]
- Who Loosens the Rope[353]
- Who Makes Wesir Young[354]
- Who Makes the Writing of the Books[355]
- Who Presides on the Temple[356]
- Who Protects Her Brother[357]
- Who Protects Her Brother Wesir[358]
- Who Records the Kingship for the Son of Aset[359]
- Who Separates Ma'at From Injustice[360]
- With the Beautiful Build/Construction[361]
- With Excellent Magic[362]
- With Her Books[363]
- With a Wide Seat in the House of the Sed Festivals[364]
- Without Another Except For Her[365]
- Writer of the *sed*-Festivals of Ra[366]
- Your Mother Seshat Clothes You[367]

---

[351] Richter, Barbara A., The Theology of Hathor of Dendera: Aural and Visual Scribal Techniques in the Per-Wer Sanctuary, (Lockwood Press, 2016), 503.

[352] Budde, Dagmar. *Die Göttin Seschat*. (H. Wodtke & K. Stegbauer, 2000), 206. Footnote 52.

[353] Budde, Dagmar. *Die Göttin Seschat*. (H. Wodtke & K. Stegbauer, 2000), 27.

[354] Budde, Dagmar. *Die Göttin Seschat*. (H. Wodtke & K. Stegbauer, 2000), 166.

[355] Budde, Dagmar. *Die Göttin Seschat*. (H. Wodtke & K. Stegbauer, 2000), 73.

[356] Hafez, Noha Mohamed. "The Scenes of Sefkhet-Abwy at The Temples". *Journal of Association of Arab Universities for Tourism and Hospitality*, 21, 1, 2021, 7.

[357] Budde, Dagmar. *Die Göttin Seschat*. (H. Wodtke & K. Stegbauer, 2000), 166. Seshat-Aset.

[358] Altenmüller, Hartwig. "Seschat,'die den Leichnam versorgt', als Herrin über Vergangenheit und Geschichte." In Z. Hawass, P. Der Manuelian, R. B. Hussein (Hg.), *Perspectives on Ancient Egypt. Studies in Honor of Edward Brovarski*, Supplément aux Annales du Service des Antiquités de l'Egypte 40, Kairo 2010, S.: 38.

[359] Budde, Dagmar. *Die Göttin Seschat*. (H. Wodtke & K. Stegbauer, 2000), 123.

[360] Budde, Dagmar. *Die Göttin Seschat*. (H. Wodtke & K. Stegbauer, 2000), 158.

[361] Budde, Dagmar. *Die Göttin Seschat*. (H. Wodtke & K. Stegbauer, 2000), 196.

[362] Budde, Dagmar. *Die Göttin Seschat*. (H. Wodtke & K. Stegbauer, 2000), 146.

[363] Budde, Dagmar. *Die Göttin Seschat*. (H. Wodtke & K. Stegbauer, 2000), 200.

[364] Budde, Dagmar. *Die Göttin Seschat*. (H. Wodtke & K. Stegbauer, 2000), 120.

[365] Richter, Barbara A., The Theology of Hathor of Dendera: Aural and Visual Scribal Techniques in the Per-Wer Sanctuary, (Lockwood Press, 2016), 341.

[366] Wainwright, G. A. "Seshat and the Pharaoh." in *The Journal of Egyptian Archaeology*, v.26 (February 1941): 35.

Titles of Seshat as Sefkhet-Abwy

- Daughter of Wesir[368]
- First of Builders[369]
- First of Heseret (Necropolis of Hermopolis Magna)[370]
- First of the Library[371]
- Foremost in the Library[372]
- Lady of the Library[373]
- Lady of the Sky[374]
- Lady of the Walls[375]
- Lady of Writing[376]
- Lady of Years[377]
- Mistress of the Great God[378]
- Mistress of the Library[379]
- Mistress of the Tongue Which Acts Against Poison[380]

---

[367] Butler, Edward. Goddesses and Gods of the Ancient Egyptians: A Theological Encyclopedia: Kindle Edition. (Phaidra Editions, 2021), 278. In Coffin Texts Spell 10.

[369] Budde, Dagmar. *Die Göttin Seschat*. (H. Wodtke & K. Stegbauer, 2000), 25.

[370] Budde, Dagmar. *Die Göttin Seschat*. (H. Wodtke & K. Stegbauer, 2000), 61.

[371] Budde, Dagmar. *Die Göttin Seschat*. (H. Wodtke & K. Stegbauer, 2000), 25.

[372] Translated from Hafez, Noha Mohamed. "The Scenes of Sefkhet-Abwy at The Temples". *Journal of Association of Arab Universities for Tourism and Hospitality*, 21, 1, 2021, 3.

[373] Hafez, Noha Mohamed. "The Scenes of Sefkhet-Abwy at The Temples". *Journal of Association of Arab Universities for Tourism and Hospitality*, 21, 1, 2021, 5.

[374] Hafez, Noha Mohamed. "The Scenes of Sefkhet-Abwy at The Temples". *Journal of Association of Arab Universities for Tourism and Hospitality*, 21, 1, 2021, 4.

[375] Siuda, Tamara L. Ancient Egyptian Daybook. (Stargazer Design, 2016), 99.

[376] Budde, Dagmar. *Die Göttin Seschat*. (H. Wodtke & K. Stegbauer, 2000), 25.

[377] Budde, Dagmar. *Die Göttin Seschat*. (H. Wodtke & K. Stegbauer, 2000), 21. Footnote 124.

[378] Hafez, Noha Mohamed. "The Scenes of Sefkhet-Abwy at The Temples". *Journal of Association of Arab Universities for Tourism and Hospitality*, 21, 1, 2021, 2.

[379] Translated from Hafez, Noha Mohamed. "The Scenes of Sefkhet-Abwy at The Temples". *Journal of Association of Arab Universities for Tourism and Hospitality*, 21, 1, 2021, 5.

[380] Budde, Dagmar. *Die Göttin Seschat*. (H. Wodtke & K. Stegbauer, 2000), 224.

- Mistress of Writing[381]
- Mistress of the Writings[382]
- Preeminent in the Scroll House[383]
- Princess of the House of Books[384]
- Princess of Library[385]
- Princess of Writing[386]
- Overseer of the House[387]
- Seven-Horned (*Sefkhet-abwy*)[388]
- Seven-Horned, Lady of the Walls[389]
- She Gives All Life, All Power[390]
- She Gives All Life to the King of Upper and Lower Egypt[391]
- She Gives Life, Stability, Power, and Many Great Jubilees[392]
- She Who Gives the Writings of Millions of Years[393]
- Who Has Lost Her Reunited Father[394]
- Who is Foremost in the Library[395]

---

[381] Hafez, Noha Mohamed. "The Scenes of Sefkhet-Abwy at The Temples". *Journal of Association of Arab Universities for Tourism and Hospitality*, 21, 1, 2021, 2.

[382] Budde, Dagmar. *Die Göttin Seschat*. (H. Wodtke & K. Stegbauer, 2000), 127.

[383] Hafez, Noha Mohamed. "The Scenes of Sefkhet-Abwy at The Temples". *Journal of Association of Arab Universities for Tourism and Hospitality*, 21, 1, 2021, 3.

[384] Budde, Dagmar. *Die Göttin Seschat*. (H. Wodtke & K. Stegbauer, 2000), 177-178

[385] Budde, Dagmar. *Die Göttin Seschat*. (H. Wodtke & K. Stegbauer, 2000), 25.

[386] Budde, Dagmar. *Die Göttin Seschat*. (H. Wodtke & K. Stegbauer, 2000), 25.

[387] Hafez, Noha Mohamed. "The Scenes of Sefkhet-Abwy at The Temples". *Journal of Association of Arab Universities for Tourism and Hospitality*, 21, 1, 2021, 11.

[388] Siuda, Tamara L. *Ancient Egyptian Daybook.* (Stargazer Design, 2016), 99.

[389] Siuda, Tamara L. *Ancient Egyptian Daybook.* (Stargazer Design, 2016), 99.

[390] Hafez, Noha Mohamed. "The Scenes of Sefkhet-Abwy at The Temples". *Journal of Association of Arab Universities for Tourism and Hospitality*, 21, 1, 2021, 2.

[391] Hafez, Noha Mohamed. "The Scenes of Sefkhet-Abwy at The Temples". *Journal of Association of Arab Universities for Tourism and Hospitality*, 21, 1, 2021, 6.

[392] Hafez, Noha Mohamed. "The Scenes of Sefkhet-Abwy at The Temples". *Journal of Association of Arab Universities for Tourism and Hospitality*, 21, 1, 2021, 5. Added the "and" for clarity.

[393] Hafez, Noha Mohamed. "The Scenes of Sefkhet-Abwy at The Temples". *Journal of Association of Arab Universities for Tourism and Hospitality*, 21, 1, 2021, 3.

[394] Budde, Dagmar. *Die Göttin Seschat*. (H. Wodtke & K. Stegbauer, 2000), 177-178.

[395] Hafez, Noha Mohamed. "The Scenes of Sefkhet-Abwy at The Temples". *Journal of Association of Arab Universities for Tourism and Hospitality*, 21, 1, 2021, 3.

Titles of Seshat-Nebet Het (Seshat-Nephthys)

Ancient Egyptian Names
- Kherseket—She Who Wipes Away Tears[396]
- Merkhetes—She Whose Flame is Painful[397]

English Names
- The Great[398]
- Great Lady[399]
- Great of Magic[400]
- Inscribes thy Kingship for All Eternity[401]
- Lady of Books[402]
- Lady of Builders[403]
- Lady of the Entire Library[404]

---

[396] El-Saghir, Mohamed and Dominique Valbelle. "Komir. I. - The Discovery of Komir Temple. Preliminary Report. II. - Deux hymnes aux divinités de Komir : Anoukis et Nephthys." *BIFAO 83* (1983), p. 164-166. Thank you to Rev. Dr. Tamara L. Siuda for this translation of Kher-seket. El-Tonssy, Mohamed A. "The Goddess Rattawy in Greco-Roman Temples." In *The Fifteen Conference Book of the General of Arab Archaeologists*, (2012-2013), pp. 199. I changed the spelling of "Kheresket" to "Kherseket".

[397] Butler, Edward P. "Opening the Way of Writing: Semiotic Metaphysics in the Book of Thoth." In *Practicing Gnosis*, (Brill, 2013), pp. 229.

[398] El-Saghir, Mohamed and Dominique Valbelle. "Komir. I. - The Discovery of Komir Temple. Preliminary Report. II. - Deux hymnes aux divinités de Komir : Anoukis et Nephthys." *BIFAO 83* (1983), p. 164-166. Translated by Chelsea Bolton.

[399] Faulkner, R. O. The Ancient Egyptian Coffin Texts Vol 1-3. Translated by R. O. Faulkner. England: Aris & Phillips, Ltd., 2004), 304. CT 778.

[400] El-Saghir, Mohamed and Dominique Valbelle. "Komir. I. - The Discovery of Komir Temple. Preliminary Report. II. - Deux hymnes aux divinites de Komir: Anoukis et Nephthys." *BIFAO 83* (1983), p. 164-166.

[401] Wainwright, Gerald A. "Seshat and the Pharaoh." *The Journal of Egyptian Archaeology* 26, no. 1 (1941): 33.

[402] Siuda, Tamara L. Nebt Het: Lady of the House. (Stargazer Design, 2010), 11.

[403] Faulkner, R. O. The Ancient Egyptian Pyramid Texts. London: Oxford University Press, 1998), 119. PT 364. Siuda, Tamara L. Nebt Het: Lady of the House. (Stargazer Design, 2010), 11.

- Lady of Writing[405]
- Mistress of Men[406]
- Mistress of Potters[407]
- Mistress of Writing[408]
- Possessor of Life in the Night-Bark[409]
- Princess of the House of Life[410]
- Sister of God[411]
- Small Seshat[412]
- Twin Sisters (Seshat and Mafdet; Aset and Nebet Het)[413]
- Who Commands the Divine Decrees[414]
- Who Controls the Temples[415]
- Who Raises up Heru[416]

---

[404] El-Saghir, Mohamed and Dominique Valbelle. "Komir. I. - The Discovery of Komir Temple. Preliminary Report. II. - Deux hymnes aux divinités de Komir : Anoukis et Nephthys." *BIFAO 83* (1983), p. 164-166. Translated by Chelsea Bolton.

[405] El-Saghir, Mohamed and Dominique Valbelle. "Komir. I. - The Discovery of Komir Temple. Preliminary Report. II. - Deux hymnes aux divinités de Komir : Anoukis et Nephthys." *BIFAO 83* (1983), p. 164-166. Translated by Chelsea Bolton.

[406] El-Saghir, Mohamed and Dominique Valbelle. "Komir. I. - The Discovery of Komir Temple. Preliminary Report. II. - Deux hymnes aux divinites de Komir : Anoukis et Nephthys." *BIFAO 83* (1983), p. 164-166.

[407] Faulkner, R. O. The Ancient Egyptian Coffin Texts Vol 1-3. Translated by R. O. Faulkner. England: Aris & Phillips, Ltd., 2004), 304. CT 778.

[408] De Wit, Constant. *Les Inscriptions du Temple d'Opet a Karnak III: Traduction integrale des textes rituels-Essai d'interpretation.* (Bruxelles : Edition de la Fondation Egyptologique Reine Elisabeth, 1968), 80.

[409] Faulkner, R. O. The Ancient Egyptian Coffin Texts Vol 1-3. Translated by R. O. Faulkner. England: Aris & Phillips, Ltd., 2004), 304. CT 778.

[410] Budde, Dagmar. *Die Göttin Seschat.* (H. Wodtke & K. Stegbauer, 2000), 216.

[411] De Wit, Constant. *Les Inscriptions du Temple d'Opet a Karnak III: Traduction integrale des textes rituels-Essai d'interpretation.* (Bruxelles : Edition de la Fondation Egyptologique Reine Elisabeth, 1968), 80.

[412] Budde, Dagmar. *Die Göttin Seschat.* (H. Wodtke & K. Stegbauer, 2000), 216.

[413] Westendorf, Wolfhart. "Beiträge aus und zu den medizinischen Texten." *Zeitschrift für ägyptische Sprache und Altertumskunde* 92, no. 1 (1966): 136.

[414] El-Saghir, Mohamed and Dominique Valbelle. "Komir. I. - The Discovery of Komir Temple. Preliminary Report. II. - Deux hymnes aux divinites de Komir : Anoukis et Nephthys." *BIFAO 83* (1983), p. 164-166.

[415] De Wit, Constant. *Les Inscriptions du Temple d'Opet a Karnak III: Traduction integrale des textes rituels-Essai d'interpretation.* (Bruxelles : Edition de la Fondation Egyptologique Reine Elisabeth, 1968), 80.

[416] Faulkner, R. O. The Ancient Egyptian Coffin Texts Vol 1-3. Translated by R. O. Faulkner.

- Who Resides in the House of the Archivists[417]
- With the Excellent Heart[418]

England: Aris & Phillips, Ltd., 2004), 304. CT 778.

[417] El-Saghir, Mohamed and Dominique Valbelle. "Komir. I. - The Discovery of Komir Temple. Preliminary Report. II. - Deux hymnes aux divinites de Komir : Anoukis et Nephthys." *BIFAO 83* (1983), p. 164-166.

[418] Budde, Dagmar. *Die Göttin Seschat*. (H. Wodtke & K. Stegbauer, 2000), 216.

Seshat's Identification with Other Gods

- Aset (Isis)
- Hethert (Hathor)
- Ma'at
- Mut
- Nebet Het (Nephthys)
- Nit (Neith)
- Raettawy (Raittawy)
- Shai
- Sopdet (Sothis, Sirius)
- Tefnut[419]

---

[419] Pereira, Ronaldo Guilherme Gurgel. "Some Remarks on the Book of Thoth: concerning Seshat, Shai and the 'invention'of the Hermetic Agathos Daimon." In *International Congress for Young Egyptologists*, vol. 25, 2012, 49 and 50.
Belmonte, Juan Antonio, Miguel Ángel Molinero Polo, and Noemi Miranda. "Unveiling Seshat: New insights into the stretching of the cord ceremony." *In Search of Cosmic Order: Selected Essays on Egyptian Archaeoastronomy* (2009): 204. Sauneron, Serge, *Esna V: Les fêtes religieuses d'Esna aux derniers siècles du paganisme,* (Cairo: IFAO, 1962; 2004), 289-291.

Ancient and Modern Sacred Symbols

- Accounting Ledgers
- Books and E-Books
- Computers
- Cosmetics
- Emblem of Seshat (Hieroglyph of Seshat)[420]
- Instrument Used in the Stretching of the Cord Ceremony
- Library
- Legal Record Keeping
- Palm Branches
- Papyrus
- Pen and Paper
- Scrolls
- Star[421]
- Stylus and Reed Pen
- Tablets
- Typewriter
- Persea Tree (Tree of Life; World Tree)[422]
- Writing Implements

Sacred Animals
- Dog[423]

---

[420] Hafez, Noha Mohamed. "The Scenes of Sefkhet-Abwy at The Temples". *Journal of Association of Arab Universities for Tourism and Hospitality*, 21, 1, 2021, 1.

[421] Hafez, Noha Mohamed. "The Scenes of Sefkhet-Abwy at The Temples". *Journal of Association of Arab Universities for Tourism and Hospitality*, 21, 1, 2021, 1.

[422] Hafez, Noha Mohamed. "The Scenes of Sefkhet-Abwy at The Temples". *Journal of Association of Arab Universities for Tourism and Hospitality*, 21, 1, 2021, 1.

[423] Butler, Edward P. "Opening the Way of Writing: Semiotic Metaphysics in the Book of Thoth." In *Practicing Gnosis*, (Brill, 2013), pp. 248.

- Leopard (Panther)

Sacred Days

Chronokrater Days are days that are watched over or guarded by certain Gods and Goddesses.

No Dates Recorded—Birthday of Seshat and Mafdet[424]

3rd Akhet/Hethara/October
11—Chronokrater: Seshat, Seven-Horned, Lady of the Walls[425]
12—Chronokrater: Seshat, Seven-Horned, Lady of the Walls[426]
23—Feast of Seshat[427]

1 Peret/Tybi/December
19 of 1 Peret to 2 Peret 4 (Solstice)—Feast of the Return of the Wandering Eye Goddess[428]

2 Peret/Mechir/January
4—Feast of the Return of the Wandering Eye Goddess[429]

1 Shomu/Pachons/April
25—Chronokrater: Seshat, Mistress of the Wall(s)[430]

---

[424] Westendorf, Wolfhart. "Beiträge aus und zu den medizinischen Texten." *Zeitschrift für ägyptische Sprache und Altertumskunde* 92, no. 1 (1966): 136.

[425] Siuda, Tamara L. Ancient Egyptian Daybook. (Stargazer Design, 2016), 99.

[426] Siuda, Tamara L. Ancient Egyptian Daybook. (Stargazer Design, 2016), 99.

[427] Siuda, Tamara L. Ancient Egyptian Daybook. (Stargazer Design, 2016), 104.

[428] Siuda, Tamara L. The Ancient Egyptian Daybook. (Stargazer Design, 2016), 137, 141-142 and 153. Levai, Jessica. Aspects of the Goddess Nephthys, Especially During the Graeco-Roman Period in Egypt. (Rhode Island: Brown University Dissertation, 2007), 61-62.

[429] Siuda, Tamara L. The Ancient Egyptian Daybook. (Stargazer Design, 2016), 137, 141-142 and 153. Levai, Jessica. Aspects of the Goddess Nephthys, Especially During the Graeco-Roman Period in Egypt. (Rhode Island: Brown University Dissertation, 2007), 61-62.

[430] Siuda, Tamara L. Ancient Egyptian Daybook. (Stargazer Design, 2016), 238.

3 Shomu/Epiphi/June
Solstice—Departure of the Wandering Goddess[431]

[431] Siuda, Tamara L. The Ancient Egyptian Daybook. (Stargazer Design, 2016), 137, 140-142 and
. Levai, Jessica. Aspects of the Goddess Nephthys, Especially During the Graeco-Roman
Period in Egypt. (Rhode Island: Brown University Dissertation, 2007), 61-62.

Shrine of Seshat

Items

- Image or Statue of Seshat
- White or Panther or Leopard Print Altar Cloth
- Writing Implements
- Candle or LED Candle
- Lighter
- Bowl with water
- Incense or Essential Oil or Cologne Spirit Waters
- *The Oracle of Seshet* by Rev. Normandi Ellis and A. Auset Rohn (optional)

Scent

- Florida Water Cologne
- Frankincense
- Patchouli
- Myrrh

Colors

- Gold
- Leopard Print
- Purple
- White

Offerings

- Beef
- Beer
- Bread
- Chicken

- Chocolate
- Coffee
- Duck
- Fruit
- Lemonade
- Lemon Cake
- Mead
- Milk
- Milk with Honey
- Tea
- Vegetables
- Water
- White Wine
- Wine

Non-Edible Offerings
- Blank Journals
- Building Tools
- Flowers
- Jewelry
- Pens or Pencils

Prayer Ideas
- Architecture
- Astronomy
- Astrology
- Beauty
- Books
- Book Keeping
- Book Stores
- Cleaning Home or Office
- Cosmetics
- Creative Writing

- Learning
- Librarian and Libraries
- Mathematics
- Organizing Home or Office
- Reading
- Record Keeping
- Schoolwork
- Science
- Set Up a Shrine ("Temple Building")
- Wisdom
- Writing

Gods and Goddesses Name List

- Aset, Auset, Iset (Isis)
- Bast, Bastet
- Djehuty, Tehuti (Thoth)
- Hethert, Hetharu; Hwt Hrw (Hathor)
- Heru-pa-Khered (Horus the Child; Harpocrates; Harpokrates)
- Heru-sa-Aset (Horus, son of Isis; Horus, the Younger; Harsiese)
- Heru Wer (Horus, the Great; Horus, the Elder; Haroeris)
- Menhyt (Menhit)
- Mut, Mout (Muth)
- Nebet Het, Nebt-Het; Nebet Hwt (Nephthys)
- Nebetuu (Nebtu)
- Nit, Net (Neith)
- Raet, Raettawy (Raittawy, Rattawy)
- Sekhmet (Sachmis)
- Seshat, Seshet, Sesheta, Seschat
- Set, Sutekh (Seth)
- Sobek, Sebek (Suchos)
- Sopdet (Sothis; Sirius)
- Tefnut, Tefenet
- Wenut, Unut
- Wepwawet, Upuaut (Ophois)
- Wesir, Ausar, Asar (Osiris)
- Yinepu, Anpu, Inpu (Anubis)

Bibliography

Altenmüller, Hartwig. "Zum Ursprung von Isis und Nephthys." *Studien zur altägyptischen Kultur* (1999): 1-26.

Altenmüller, Hartwig. "Seschat,'die den Leichnam versorgt', als Herrin über Vergangenheit und Geschichte." In Z. Hawass, P. Der Manuelian, R. B. Hussein (Hg.), *Perspectives on Ancient Egypt. Studies in Honor of Edward Brovarski*, Supplément aux Annales du Service des Antiquités de l'Egypte 40, Kairo 2010, S.: 35-52.

Belmonte, Juan Antonio, Miguel Ángel Molinero Polo, and Noemi Miranda. "Unveiling Seshat: New insights into the stretching of the cord ceremony." *In Search of Cosmic Order: Selected Essays on Egyptian Archaeoastronomy* (2009): 195-212.

Budde, Dagmar. *Die Göttin Seschat*. H. Wodtke & K. Stegbauer, 2000.

Butler, Edward. Goddesses and Gods of the Ancient Egyptians: A Theological Encyclopedia: Kindle Edition. Phaidra Editions, 2021.

Butler, Edward P. "Opening the Way of Writing: Semiotic Metaphysics in the Book of Thoth." In *Practicing Gnosis*, Brill, 2013, pp. 215-247.

Cauville, Sylvie, Le Temple de Dendara: La Porte d'Isis, Dendara. Cairo: IFAO, 1999.

Cauville, Sylvie. Dendara. Le temple d'Isis. Vol. II: Analyse a la lumiere du temple d'Hathor. Peeters, 2009.

De Wit, Constant. *Les Inscriptions du Temple d'Opet a Karnak III: Traduction integrale des textes rituels-Essai d'interpretation.* (Bruxelles : Edition de la Fondation Egyptologique Reine Elisabeth, 1968.

Dunand, Francoise. Le Culte D'Isis Et Les Ptolémées. Netherlands: Brill, 2015.

El-Saghir, Mohamed and Dominique Valbelle. "Komir. I. - The Discovery of Komir Temple. Preliminary Report. II. - Deux hymnes aux divinités de Komir : Anoukis et Nephthys." *BIFAO 83.* (1983), pp. 149-170.

El-Tonssy, Mohamed A. "The Goddess Rattawy in the Greco-Roman Temples" الإلهة رعت تاوى فى معابد العصر اليونانى الرومانى". *The Conference Book of the General Union of Arab Archeologists. 15.* (2012), pp. 188-214.

Faulkner, R. O. The Ancient Egyptian Pyramid Texts. London: Oxford University Press, 1998.

Faulkner, R. O. The Ancient Egyptian Coffin Texts Vol 1-3. England: Aris & Phillips, Ltd., 2004.

Faulkner, R. O. The Ancient Egyptian Coffin Texts Vol 1: Spells 1-354. England: Aris & Phillips, Ltd, 1973.

Faulkner, R. O. The Ancient Egyptian Coffin Texts Vol 2: Spells 355-787. England: Aris & Phillips, Ltd, 1977.

Faulkner, R. O. The Ancient Egyptian Coffin Texts Vol 3: Spells 788-1185. England: Aris & Phillips, Ltd, 1978.

Hafez, Noha Mohamed. "The Scenes of Sefkhet-Abwy at The Temples". *Journal of Association of Arab Universities for Tourism and Hospitality,* 21, 1, 2021, 1-24. doi: 10.21608/jaauth.2021.84216.1200

Jasnow, Richard, and Karl-Theodor Zauzich. The Ancient Egyptian Book of Thoth: A Demotic Discourse on Knowledge and Pendant to the Classical Hermetica. Wiesbaden: Harrassowitz Verlag, 2005.

Kockelmann, Holger and Erich Winter. Philae III: Die Zweite Ostkolonnade des Tempels der Isis in Philae. (CO II und CO II K). Verlag der Osterreichischen Akademie der Wissenschaften/Austrian Academy of Sciences, 2016.

Kurth, Dieter. *Edfou VII. Vol. 1-2.* Otto Harrassowitz Verlag, 2004.

Leitz, Christian, and Dagmar Budde, et. al. Lexikon der Ägyptischen Götter und Götterbezeichnungen (LGG, OLA 129, Band 8). Peeters, 2003.

Levai, Jessica. Aspects of the Goddess Nephthys, Especially During the Greaco-Roman Period in Egypt. Rhode Island: Brown University Dissertation, 2007.

Magdolen, Dušan. "The Development of the Sign of the Ancient Egyptian Goddess Seshat Down to the End of the Old Kingdom: Analysis and Interpretation." Asian and African Studies 15, no. 1 (2006): 55-72.

Magdolen, Dusan. "A New Investigation of the Symbol of Ancient Egyptian Goddess Seshat." in Asian and African Studies, v.18 no.2 (12/2009): 169-189.

Pereira, Ronaldo Guilherme Gurgel. "Some Remarks on the Book of Thoth: concerning Seshat, Shai and the 'invention'of the Hermetic Agathos Daimon." In International Congress for Young Egyptologists, vol. 25, 2012, 49-55.

Pinch, Geraldine. Egyptian Mythology: A Guide to the Gods, Goddesses and Traditions of Ancient Egypt. New York: Oxford University Press, 2004.

Richter, Barbara A., The Theology of Hathor of Dendera: Aural and Visual Scribal Techniques in the Per-Wer Sanctuary, Lockwood Press, 2016.

Sauneron, Serge, Esna V: Les fêtes religieuses d'Esna aux derniers siècles du paganisme, (Cairo: IFAO, 1962; 2004.

Schneider, Thomas. "Das Schriftzeichen "Rosette" und die Göttin Seschat." Studien zur Altägyptischen Kultur 24 (1997), 241-267

Siuda, Tamara L. Nebt-Het: Lady of the House. Illinois: Stargazer Design, 2010.

Siuda, Tamara L. The Ancient Egyptian Prayerbook. Illinois: Stargazer Design, 2009.

Siuda, Tamara L. The Ancient Egyptian Daybook. Stargazer Design, 2016.

Wainwright, G. A. "Seshat and the Pharaoh." in *The Journal of Egyptian Archaeology, v.26* (February 1941): 30-40.

Wainwright, G. A. "Seshat's nš-Shrine." in *The Journal of Egyptian Archaeology, v.25 no.1* (1939): 104.

Westendorf, Wolfhart. "Beiträge aus und zu den medizinischen Texten." *Zeitschrift für ägyptische Sprache und Altertumskunde* 92, no. 1 (1966): 128-164.

Wilkinson, Richard H. The Complete Gods and Goddesses of Ancient Egypt. London: Thames and Hudson, 2003.

About the Author

Chelsea Luellon Bolton has a BA and MA in Religious Studies from the University of South Florida. She is the author of *Lady of Praise, Lady of Power: Ancient Hymns of the Goddess Aset*; *Queen of the Road: Poetry of the Goddess Aset*; and *Magician, Mother and Queen: A Research Paper on the Goddess Aset*. Her other books are *Lord of Strength and Power: Ancient Hymns for Wepwawet* and *Sun, Star and Desert Sand: Poems for the Egyptian Gods*. She is the editor and a contributor of the anthology *She Who Speaks Through Silence: An Anthology for Nephthys*. Her other latest books are *Mother of Magic: Ancient Hymns for Aset*; *Flaming Lioness: Ancient Hymns for Egyptian Goddesses*; and *Lady of the Temple: Ancient Hymns for Nephthys*. Her poetry has been previously published in various anthologies. She lives with tons of books. You can find more of her work at her blog address: http://fiercelybrightone.com

Website:
https://fiercelybrightone.com/

Other Books by Chelsea Luellon Bolton

Ancient Hymns Collections
- Lady of Praise, Lady of Power: Ancient Hymns of the Goddess Aset.
- Mother of Magic: Ancient Hymns for Aset.
- Lady of the Temple: Ancient Hymns for Nephthys.
- Lady of Water and Flame: Ancient Hymns for Tefnut.
- Solar Lioness: Ancient Hymns for Sekhmet.
- Mother of Writing: Ancient Hymns for Seshat.
- Lord of Strength and Power: Ancient Hymns for Wepwawet.
- Flaming Lioness: Ancient Hymns for Egyptian Goddesses.
- Two Horizons: Ancient Hymns for Egyptian Gods.
- Beauty and Strength: Ancient Hymns for Egyptian Gods.

Anthologies
- Queen of the Hearth: An Anthology for Frigga.
- She Who Speaks Through Silence: An Anthology for Nephthys.
- Solar Flares and Sunbeams: An Anthology for Ra.
- Lord of the Ways: An Anthology for Wepwawet.
- Mother of Nine: An Anthology for Oya.
- Sweet of Love: An Anthology for Bast and Bast-Mut.
- Lady of Arrows: An Anthology for Neith.
- Thrice Great Goddess: An Anthology for Aset.

Research Papers
- Magician, Mother and Queen: A Research Paper on the Goddess Aset.
- Holy Mother, Healer, and Queen: Papers on the Feminine Divine.

Modern Poetry
- Queen of the Road: Poetry of the Goddess Aset.
- Divine Words, Divine Praise: Poetry for the Divine Powers.
- Divine Beings, Earthly Praise: Poems for Divine Powers.
- Sun, Star and Desert Sand: Poems for the Egyptian Gods.
- River, Star and Sky: Poems for the Egyptian Gods.

Made in the USA
Middletown, DE
12 August 2024

58992397R00071